How We Got the Bible

By Kyle Pope

How We Got the Bible

By Kyle Pope

© **Truth Publications, Inc. 2019. Second Printing.** All rights reserved. No part of this book may be reproduced in any form without written permission from the publisher. Printed in the United States of America.

First printing, 2010

All graphics and photos not done by the author were taken from the public domain.

ISBN:1-58427-298-8
ISBN: 978-158427-298-4

Truth Publications, Inc.
CEI Bookstore
220 S. Marion St., Athens, AL 35611
855-492-6657
sales@truthpublications.com
www.truthbooks.com

Contents

Introduction 1

I. Divine Inspiration 3

II. The Formation of the Old Testament 5

III. The Formation of the New Testament 23

IV. The History of the English Bible 42

V. Manuscript Discoveries and
    Modern Translations 61

Appendix: Choosing a Translation 82

Index 94

Scripture Index 97

Select Bibliography 99

A special word of thanks is due to the elders of the Olsen Park church of Christ: Ken Ford, Charles Kelley, and Patrick Ledbetter. In 2007, at their request, this study was first prepared and presented to the congregation. Shortly afterwards the material was organized into its present form.

Introduction

The Bible is the most important book in history. It has influenced billions of people throughout the ages. Laws have been fashioned upon its teachings, nations have been established upon its principles, and human souls have rested upon its promises. Yet, how is it that this book came to us? How was it transmitted from the mind of God to the hands of man? What process led to the formation of this wonderful book that we have before us?

In considering the question of how we got the Bible, we should recognize that this is not a question that is unique to the Bible. We could consider in history or literature studies on how the writings of Shakespeare were preserved. The historian or the political scientist might consider how the constitution was developed from the Magna Carta and other efforts into the great monument of liberty that defines our nation. What is different about the Bible is the fact that it presents to mankind answers that no other text can offer. As a result, understanding its transmission to man is not just the isolated study of secluded scholars, but it should concern all people because so much rests upon the validity and reliability of the biblical text.

In this study, we look at what is known about this process. We will look at both the Old and the New Testaments to consider what is understood about the formation of Scripture. We will look at the dramatic history of the Bible coming into English. Then, we will end our study with a consideration of how modern discoveries

How We Got the Bible

of biblical manuscripts have affected today's translations. Lord willing, our study will bolster faith and help to overcome doubts. It is my prayer that this study will strengthen the reader against the assaults of the enemy and grant to him or her a greater confidence in the Bible as the complete, inerrant, and wholly inspired word of God.

Kyle Pope
Amarillo, TX
kmpope@att.net

Divine Inspiration

We must start our consideration of this subject with a clear understanding of what is at issue. Either the Bible is the word of God, or it is a man-made piece of literature that has led to the death, persecution, and life upheaval of all of mankind. There can be no middle-ground. The Bible does not offer an indefinite appraisal of itself. It makes clear declarations throughout that it is from God.

Bible Claims of Inspiration

Paul told Timothy, *"All Scripture is given by inspiration of God, and is profitable for doctrine, for reproof, for correction, for instruction in righteousness, that the man of God may be complete, thoroughly equipped for every good work"* (2 Tim. 3:16, 17, NKJV). Peter declared, *"...No Prophecy of Scripture is of any private interpretation, for prophecy never came by the will of man, but holy men of God spoke as they were moved by the Holy Spirit"* (2 Pet. 1:20-21). Paul told the Christians in Thessalonica, *"For this reason we also thank God without ceasing, because when you received the word of God which you heard from us, you welcomed it not as the word of men, but as it is in truth, the word of God, which also effectively works in you who believe"* (1 Thess. 2:13). Such assertions leave no doubt that those who penned Scripture were claiming to do so by the inspiration of God.

The Nature of Inspiration

This claim of "inspiration" is more than the emotional motivation an artist might draw from a beautiful scene of nature.

How We Got the Bible

It is a claim to have been directly influenced and produced by God. René Pache in his book, *The Inspiration and Authority of Scripture*, found phrases in the Bible such as, "Thus says the Lord" or "The word of the Lord came to _____" 3808 times (65, 81).

The nature of inspiration has been described with a number of names. The inspiration of the Bible involved:

• **Plenary "Full" Inspiration.** From the Latin word *plenus*, meaning "full," plenary inspiration describes the fact that all of Scripture is inspired.

• **Verbal Inspiration.** Every word of Scripture is inspired. Not only the words of Jesus, but all of the writers of Scripture were led in the very words that they used to produce Scripture.

• **Dynamic Inspiration.** Although the personality and environment of the writer were allowed to show through, the Holy Spirit held absolute control over the outcome. As a result, when the words of Scripture were penned, it was in fact God speaking through these inspired writers to reveal His word.

Each of these descriptions address some true aspect of the nature of biblical inspiration. The Bible is wholly inspired in every word and phrase. It was revealed under the control of the Holy Spirit working through men of freewill and individual personality.

Discussion Questions
1. What are some statements the Bible makes about itself which show that it claims to be inspired of God?
2. What is meant by the three different terms that describe inspiration?

The Formation of the Old Testament

We cannot understand the process of the transmission of the Biblical text without first considering the tools that were available to biblical writers. To do this we need to briefly consider what is known about the written language that God used to communicate His word.

The Bible was revealed in three languages. The Old Testament was written in Hebrew (with a few passages in Aramaic) and the New Testament in Koine Greek (with a few words in Aramaic). There is great evidence of Divine providence in the timing and use of these languages.

Writing Material in Scripture

While modern man has seen the computer revolutionize how we communicate with one another, the Bible was revealed at one of the earliest stages in which human beings communicated thoughts and values in written form. This was done through a few basic media:

1. Tablets – of stone or clay were impressed, engraved, or stamped. The Bible describes this media a number of times. Jeremiah writes, *"The sin of Judah is written with a pen of iron; With the point of a diamond it is engraved on the tablet of their heart, And on the horns of*

Ancient Tablet

How We Got the Bible

your altars" (Jer. 17:1). The Law of Moses records, *"And when He had made an end of speaking with him on Mount Sinai, He gave Moses two tablets of the Testimony, tablets of stone, written with the finger of God"* (Exod. 31:18).

While there were Old Testament passages that were written on tablets, none of these has been preserved. What has come down to us are...

2. Scrolls – made from *papyrus* (dried plant stalks pressed and glued together) or *parchment* (dried, scraped animal skins) sewn together and put into a roll. The Bible describes this media as well. Jeremiah wrote, *"Take a scroll of a book and write on it all the words that I have spoken to you against Israel, against Judah, and against all the nations, from the day I spoke to you, from the days of Josiah even to this day"* (Jer. 36:2).

Parchment Scroll

Papyrus Manuscript

Ezekiel writes, *"Now when I looked, there was a hand stretched out to me; and behold, a scroll of a book was in it. Then He spread it before me; and there was writing on the inside and on the outside, and written on it were lamentations and mourning and woe"* (Ezek. 2:9).

We should understand that, from what we know, a "book" in the Old Testament and (most of the New Testament) was a scroll. It would not be until Christian times that the *codex* (a bound collation of pages written on both sides) would be developed.

How We Got the Bible

Early Writing Systems.

During some times in the past, God revealed Himself to men by the spoken word alone. Yet, the fact that God chose to reveal Himself to mankind in written form at a time when man was able to communicate in writing allowed this revelation to be utilized by mankind as a whole. Consideration of the development of written communication shows just what a key moment in human history it was when God chose to reveal His word.

The first types of written communication were...

1. Ideographic (Ideas conveyed in pictographic symbols). These were of at least two types, *hieroglyphic* (in Egypt) or *cuneiform* (in Mesopotamia, Persia and the Levant).

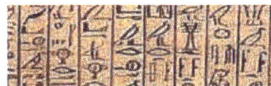
Hieroglyphics

Cuneiform

The drawbacks of either of these systems were, first their dependence upon artistic ability. Unless you could draw pictures or elaborate symbols, you couldn't be understood. A second drawback was the large number of signs needed. We can see this in the example of written Chinese—one of the only ideographic languages still in use. Chinese has been forced from time to time to simplify its written language, reducing the number of signs from 15,000 to 5,000! Can you imagine teaching elementary children 15,000 signs?

Critics of faith used to argue that the Bible's claim that the Law was given to and written down by Moses around 1400 BC was not even possible because no written, alphabetic language was then in use. This criticism is no longer even at issue. In an area near where the Israelites wandered in the wilderness of Sinai, one of the world's first alphabets has been discovered.

How We Got the Bible

2. Alphabetic writing, unlike ideographic writing is made up of graphic symbols that represent sounds. Proto-Sinaitic, thought to have been in use in the Sinai around 1500 BC, is believed to be an "ancient ancestor" of our own alphabet used in modern English. With the use of an alphabet, writing is much more accessible to the common man. In the providence of God, the first inspired writing that God revealed to man was given in the earliest stages of the use of alphabetic writing. Old Testament Hebrew may first have been revealed in this Proto-Sinaitic alphabet.

The Proto-Sinaitic Alphabet

As with all languages, the script used to write Hebrew has changed dramatically over time. We can see this by looking at how the first commandment of the Mosaic Ten Commandments could be variously written. The commandment in English reads, *"You shall have no other Gods before me"* (Exod. 20:3). If written in Proto-Sinaitic, it would have been written as shown below: Later (ca. 900 BC) it would be:

After that (700 BC):   About 100 BC it would have been:

How We Got the Bible

Finally, around 800 AD:

לא יהיה לך
אלהים
אחרים
על פני

Then with the vowels marked:

לֹא יִהְיֶה־לְךָ
אֱלֹהִים
אֲחֵרִים
עַל־פָּנָי

Although the look is different, the meaning is exactly the same: *"You shall have no other Gods before Me."*

This allows us to understand the tools the Holy Spirit led the writers of Scripture to use. Next we must consider the formation of the text itself.

Major Events for the Hebrew Text

The books of the Old Testament were revealed over a span of time from ca. 1400 BC to 400 BC. During this time 39 books were revealed to Old Testament prophets of God. There are three major biblical events that dramatically affected the formation of the text:

- *The Giving of the Law of Moses* (ca. 1400 BC).
- *The Recovery of the Book of the Law in the Reign of Josiah* (ca. 621 BC).
- *The Restoration of the Jews to Palestine and the Reforms of Ezra* (ca. 400 BC).

The Giving of the Law to Moses. After Moses led the Israelites out of Egypt, the Bible says that God revealed to him the first five books of the Old Testament. The claim is emphatic that God revealed these texts to Moses. In Leviticus we read: *"These are the commandments which the Lord commanded Moses for the children of Israel on Mount Sinai"* (Lev. 27:34). In Deuteronomy we read, *"These are the words of the covenant which the Lord*

How We Got the Bible

commanded Moses to make with the children of Israel in the land of Moab, besides the covenant which He made with them in Horeb" (Deut. 29:1). The last book of the Old Testament declares, *"Remember the Law of Moses, My servant, Which I commanded him in Horeb for all Israel, with the statutes and judgments"* (Mal. 4:4). Nehemiah writes, *"Now all the people gathered together as one man in the open square that was in front of the Water Gate and they told Ezra the scribe to bring the Book of the Law of Moses, which the LORD had commanded Israel"* (Neh. 8:1). The Bible says of itself that God gave the Law to Moses.

Man Says This Isn't True!

Unfortunately, modern man rejects these clear claims. Julius Wellhausen, a 19th century scholar influenced by the Darwinistic evolutionary thought of his day, developed a theory called the "Documentary Hypothesis." This theory claimed the Pentateuch was not given by God, or written by Moses, but was formed by man from different sources. He labeled these imagined sources: 1. *Source J* – thus named because it supposedly used the name *Jehovah* for God; 2. *Source E* – thus named because it supposedly used the name *Elohim* for God; 3. *Source D* – the so-called "Deuteronomist" source; and 4. *Source P* – the so-called "Priestly" source. These hypothetical sources, according to the theory, were then compiled together from 900-400 BC.

What Is the Truth? The Bible says the Law was written by Moses and given by God. In the Pentateuch we find the phrases...

> **"The LORD spoke to Moses"** (104 Times);
> **"The LORD said to Moses"** (56 Times);
> **"The LORD commanded Moses"** (28 Times).

The Bible Says the Law of Moses was written by Moses— *"...have you not read in the book of Moses..."* (Mark 12:26); *"Did*

How We Got the Bible

not Moses give you the law..." (John 7:19); although, it was given by God, *"The law was through Moses"* (John 1:17).

Ancient writers believed it was written by Moses. Manetho, an Egyptian Historian (ca. 240 BC) in speaking of Moses, says he was "... The man who gave them their constitution and laws" (Quoted by Josephus, *Against Apion* 1.26.4). Josephus, the Jewish Historian (ca. 80-90 AD), in speaking of the Jewish Scriptures, says they are "... justly believed to be Divine, and of them five belong to Moses, which contain his laws, and the traditions of the origins of mankind till his death" (*Against Apion* 1.8.1).

Much of the argument of the Documentary Hypothesis rests on the use of different names for God. A major problem for this theory is the fact that references to *Elohim* and *Jehovah* are found together in the Pentateuch. The phrase "LORD (*Jehovah*) God (*Elohim*)" is found 47 times (Genesis - 26; Exodus - 13; Deuteronomy - 8). The words "LORD (*Jehovah*)" and "God (*Elohim*)" in the same verse are found 413 times (Genesis - 37; Exodus - 50; Leviticus - 38; Numbers - 11; Deuteronomy - 277). Did these imagined "compilers" of the various hypothetical sources, carefully intermingle the different names for God into their composition to avoid detection?

The fact is that there is no evidence for this false theory. In spite of this, the "Documentary Hypothesis" is taught as fact in major universities all over the world. It is important for young Christians who go off to college to be aware of this and to be prepared to answer these false claims.

The next major event occurred several centuries later...

Recovery of the "Book of the Law." By the time of king Josiah, king of Judah, the Israelites had seen their people given

How We Got the Bible

to idolatry time and again. The division of nations had seen some of the Israelites conquered and deported by the Assyrians. Judah had repeatedly turned away from following God. Yet, occasionally an honorable king came to the throne and strove to do what was right. Josiah was such a king. Early in his reign the Bible says, *"Then Hilkiah the high priest said to Shaphan the scribe, 'I have found the Book of the Law in the house of the LORD.' And Hilkiah gave the book to Shaphan, and he read it"* (2 Kings 22:8). What was this "Book of the Law?" Was it a single book of the Law of Moses? Was it the entire law, spoken of as one book?

If we look in Scripture itself we find the phrase "Book of the Law" is used nineteen times in the Old Testament (Deut. 28:61; 29:21; 30:10; 31:26; Josh. 1:8; 8:31, 34; 22:11; 2 Chron. 17:9; 34:14; Neh. 8:1, 3, 18; 9:3). It is used once in the New Testament (Gal. 3:10), yet the phrase "books" of the Law is never used in Scripture. We also know that Hebrew books were usually not titled. This is seen in the famous "Isaiah Scroll," discovered among the Dead Sea Scrolls. The scroll known as 1QIsa^a (ca. 100 BC) contains no title. Modern texts of the Hebrew Bible have titles, but they do so utilizing the more recent custom of employing the first word of the text as the name.

1QIsa^a with No Title Heading

The names we know (*Genesis, Exodus, etc.*) actually come from the Greek translation of the Old Testament made before the time of Christ that was used by many Christians in the early history of the church.

How We Got the Bible

Were separate books ever combined into one scroll? The Babylonian Talmud indicates that scrolls were usually written with four lines between different books (*Baba Batra* 13b). All of this makes it clear that the "Book of the Law" was either one scroll or a group of scrolls of all five books of the Law.

The Bible goes on to say: *"Now it happened, when the king heard the words of the Book of the Law, that he tore his clothes"* (2 Kings 22:11). It is hard to imagine that the Israelites could lose the "book of the Law," but that is exactly what they did. This teaches us something important about God. While He allows man to have the freewill to turn away from Him, in His providence He always preserves His word.

The Preservation of God's Word. The Bible teaches the principle throughout, that God will preserve His word. Jesus taught, *"for assuredly, I say to you, till heaven and earth pass away, one jot or one tittle will by no means pass from the law till all is fulfilled"* (Matt. 5:18). This shows both God's preservation of His word, and Jesus' own belief that every "jot" and "tittle" of Scripture was from God. He said further, *"Heaven and earth will pass away, but My words will by no means pass away"* (Matt. 24:35). Peter wrote, through the Holy Spirit, *"...All flesh is as grass, and all the glory of man as the flower of the grass. The grass withers, and its flower falls away, but the word of the Lord endures forever..."* (1 Pet. 1:24-25). This is drawn from Isaiah's declaration, *"The grass withers, the flower fades, but the word of our God stands forever"* (Isa. 40:8). Finally, the Psalmist tells us, *"...Forever, O Lord, Your word is settled in heaven"* (Ps. 119:89). Many things may change, but God promises that He will preserve His word through all of these changes.

How We Got the Bible

Teaching and Restoration of the Law

The discovery (or recovery) of the Law, began a nationwide movement to return to faithfulness to the Lord. Scripture tells us:

> Now the king sent them to gather all the elders of Judah and Jerusalem to him. The king went up to the house of the LORD with all the men of Judah, and with him all the inhabitants of Jerusalem—the priests and the prophets and all the people, both small and great. And he read in their hearing all the words of the Book of the Covenant which had been found in the house of the LORD. Then the king stood by a pillar and made a covenant before the LORD, to follow the LORD and to keep His commandments and His testimonies and His statutes, with all his heart and all his soul, to perform the words of this covenant that were written in this book. And all the people took a stand for the covenant (2 Kings 23:1-3).

During this period, undoubtedly much was accomplished towards the restoration, publication, and preservation of the biblical books that had been revealed to that point in time. Yet, one further event occurred that affected the formation of the Old Testament...

The Restoration of Ezra

About two hundred years later, after Judah had fallen to Babylon, and many of her sons had been carried off to captivity, the Lord worked through a man named Ezra, when the Jews were allowed to return to Jerusalem under Persian rule. The Bible says, *"...Ezra came up from Babylon; and he was a skilled scribe in the Law of Moses, which the LORD God of Israel had given. The king granted him all his request, according to the hand of the LORD his God upon Him"* (Ezra 7:6). *"...For Ezra had prepared his heart to seek the Law of the LORD, and to do it, and to teach statutes and ordinances in Israel"* (Ezra 7:10). Like Josiah, he discovered that his people were unfaithful. To address this, he initiated a major period of restoration.

How We Got the Bible

The Teaching of the Law. Ezra assisted in a major return to respect for God's word. Scripture tells us:

> Now all the people gathered together as one man in the open square that was in front of the Water Gate; and they told Ezra the scribe to bring the Book of the Law of Moses, which the LORD had commanded Israel. So Ezra the priest brought the Law before the assembly of men and women and all who could hear with understanding on the first day of the seventh month. Then he read from it in the open square that was in front of the Water Gate from morning until midday, before the men and women and those who could understand; and the ears of all the people were attentive to the Book of the Law. So Ezra the scribe stood on a platform of wood which they had made for the purpose; and beside him, at his right hand, stood Mattithiah, Shema, Anaiah, Urijah, Hilkiah, and Maaseiah; and at his left hand Pedaiah, Mishael, Malchijah, Hashum, Hashbadana, Zechariah, and Meshullam. And Ezra opened the book in the sight of all the people, for he was standing above all the people; and when he opened it, all the people stood up. And Ezra blessed the LORD, the great God. Then all the people answered, "Amen, Amen!" while lifting up their hands. And they bowed their heads and worshiped the LORD with their faces to the ground. Also Jeshua, Bani, Sherebiah, Jamin, Akkub, Shabbethai, Hodijah, Maaseiah, Kelita, Azariah, Jozabad, Hanan, Pelaiah, and the Levites, helped the people to understand the Law; and the people stood in their place. So they read distinctly from the book, in the Law of God; and they gave the sense, and helped them to understand the reading (Neh. 8:1-8).

There can be little question that the events that took place during these times served to complete the body of Old Testament Scriptures, preserve them, teach them, and hand them down.

"The Great Assembly" (or "Great Synagogue") is a term used by the Jews for this group of leaders who restored the Law together with Ezra. The Jewish Mishnah claimed, "Moses received the Torah on Sinai, and handed it down to Joshua; Joshua to the elders; the elders to the prophets; and the prophets handed it down to the Men of the Great Assembly" (*Perke Aboth* 1). This period brings to an end Divine inspiration of Old Testament Scriptures. During this time (if not shortly afterwards), the Old Testament *Canon* was closed. After this, all other religious writing came to be viewed as uninspired and of lesser value. We will see an example of this later in our study.

The Old Testament Canon

The word *canon* meaning "rule, or measuring line" refers to the complete collection of Divinely inspired books. A vital issue in considering how the Bible came to us has to do with what constitutes the full body or *Canon* of Old Testament Scriptures. To address this, let's begin by looking at some issues concerning the grouping of the books and divisions of the Old Testament.

Division of the Old Testament. We divide the Old Testament into four sections based upon the age and the type of literature: Law, History, Poetry, and Prophecy. This grouping comes to us from the Greek translation of the Old Testament done before the time of Christ. We count the number of books at 39. Ancient and modern Jews divide the same books of the Hebrew Bible into three sections:

Torah - תּוֹרָה (Law)
Nevim - נְבִיאִים (Prophets)
Ketubim - כְּתוּבִים (Writings)

Ancient Jews divided the same books we have today into 22 (or sometimes 24) books. This was accomplished by counting some pairs of books as one (e.g. Judges-Ruth; 1-2 Samuel; 1-2 Kings; 1-2 Chronicles; Jeremiah-Lamentations; 12 Minor Prophets =1). 22 was changed to 24 by separating Judges & Ruth and Jeremiah & Lamentations. These divisions are very ancient and reflect how early the Old Testament canon was closed.

How We Got the Bible

Jesus accepted this grouping and acknowledged the closed Old Testament canon. Luke quoted Jesus to say, *"...These are the words which I spoke to you while I was still with you, that all things must be fulfilled which were written in the Law, the Prophets and the Psalms concerning Me"* (Luke 24:44). Psalms is the first book of the third section, the *Ketubim* (Writings). Jesus identifies this section by referring to the first book of the section. With this statement Jesus acknowledged His acceptance of all three portions of the Old Testament canon.

Witnesses to a Closed Old Testament Canon. Modern liberal scholars try to suggest that both the Old and New Testament canons were closed long after the time of their revelation. If this were true it would put man in the position of having determined what was inspired (and canonical) and what was not. These critics fail to appreciate the witness of history. At least three sources knew a "closed" canon very early. The apocryphal Book of Ecclesiasticus or Sirach (ca. 190 BC) in its prologue claims, "Many and great things have been given to us by the LAW and the PROPHETS and by OTHERS...my grandfather, Joshua, gave himself to the reading of the LAW and the PROPHETS and OTHER books of our fathers." Discussing translation of Hebrew, he speaks of "...the LAW itself, and the PROPHETS and the REST of the books " (Prologue, emphasis mine). Philo of Alexandria (ca. 30 AD) speaks of a Jewish monastic sect "...studying in that place the LAWS and the sacred oracles of God enunciated by the HOLY PROPHETS and HYMNS and PSALMS... " (*On the Contemplative Life*, 25; emphasis mine). The Jewish Historian Josephus (ca. 80-90 AD) claimed, "We have...22 books which contain the records of all the past times; which are justly believed to be Divine." He explains, "...five belong to MOSES...from the death of Moses to the reign of Artaxerxes...the PROPHETS

How We Got the Bible

wrote down what was done in thirteen books...the remaining four contain HYMNS to God and precepts for the conduct of life" (*Against Apion* 1.8.1; emphasis mine). Clearly, the canon of the Old Testament was closed before the time of Christ. In spite of this evidence some seek to look to a different period.

The "Council" of Jamnia is a theoretical Jewish "council" that liberal scholars claim closed the Old Testament canon around 100 AD, in the city of Jamnia after the destruction of Jerusalem. If this was true, not only would it put men in the position of determining what was (and was not) in the Bible, but it would leave a 500 year gap between the time in which the canon was closed and the composition of the last books. While there is some evidence that the books of Ecclesiastes and Song of Solomon were discussed during this time, the canon was closed and well established long before this. It may well have been that the intimate content of Song of Solomon and the seemingly nihilistic philosophy of Ecclesiastes were challenges to the Jews of this time. Yet, fewer and fewer scholars now see Jamnia as any type of authoritative meeting.

Did "councils" determine what was in the Bible? It is important, early in our study, to consider what bearing (if any) "councils" of men have held over the biblical text. It must be emphatically declared that councils or declarations of men did not determine what was Divine, inspired, or authoritative. At best, they have simply stated what was already understood to be true.

How We Got the Bible

The Old Testament into Greek

While the Old Testament was written in Hebrew, there was an event that occurred in the time between the Old and New Testament periods that had a significant bearing upon the Old Testament text we have today—the translation of the Old Testament into Greek.

Alexander the Great

The conquest of Alexander the Great brought the Greek language to much of the ancient world. During the reign of Ptolemy II (ca. 285-246 BC.), a Greek king over Egypt after Alexander, the Old Testament began to be translated into Greek. A work known as the *Letter of Aristeas* tells of Ptolemy using 72 Jewish scholars to make a translation of the Old Testament. The number of scholars (rounded to *seventy*) is where this work draws its name. The Greek word for "seventy," *septuaginta* gives us the name of this work, the *Septuagint* (abbreviated in Roman numerals LXX).

The Septuagint (LXX) utilized the Greek custom of naming books. For example, the name *Exodus* comes from the Greek *ex* "out of" and *hodos* "road, way," referring literally to "the way out" of Egypt. Many of the names we use are from the LXX. The arrangement we use of the books of the Old Testament (i.e. Law, History, Poetry, and Prophecy) is derived from the LXX.

Septuagint (LXX) Papyrus

How We Got the Bible

The LXX was the Old Testament of many early Christians. Some Old Testament quotes in the New Testament are directly from the LXX. While most modern translations use the Hebrew text as the basis for English translation, many of these conventions drawn from the LXX are still employed in modern editions of the Old Testament.

Extra-Canonical Books

The issue of what comprises the Old Testament canon does not rest merely in the number and division of books, but also in what comprises a canonical work and what does not. Great doubt is raised in the believer's mind if the impression is given that something might have been left out. To address this, we end this portion of our study with a consideration of two groups of *extra-canonical* (or more properly NON-canonical) texts.

Around the time of Ezra the canon was closed. Yet, many religious and historical works were produced after this period. These are divided into two groups: the *Apocrypha* (ca. 300 BC – AD 70) and the *Pseudepigrapha* (ca. 200 BC – AD 200).

The Apocrypha (ca. 300 BC – 70 AD) refers to fourteen Jewish historical and religious texts (*Maccabees, Tobit, Bel and the Dragon, Sirach, etc.*). These were viewed as uninspired supplementary readings that held no authority. Josephus, in his work *Against Apion*, says that other works after Ezra "hath not been esteemed of the like authority with the former by our forefathers because there hath not been an exact succession of prophets from that time"

How We Got the Bible

(1.8.1). The Babylonian Talmud, says Zechariah and Malachi came "at the end of the prophets" (*Baba Batra* 14b).

While these books are included in many copies of the LXX, they were probably considered supplementary material. Jesus and New Testament writers never quote from a single apocryphal book (although almost every canonical book is quoted). Even so, these books are included in Roman Catholic Bibles and were in the original 1611 *King James* Bible. While the Apocrypha may have some historical value, it is not inspired.

The Pseudepigrapha (ca. 200 BC – 200 AD) are fanciful texts written under the pseudonym of ancient writers (e.g. *Life of Adam and Eve; The Testaments of the Twelve Patriarchs; Enoch; Martyrdom and Ascension of Isaiah*). While many of these works were known among the Jews, these were like our modern works of religious fiction. They were not viewed as inspired and held no authority. In addition to scriptural and 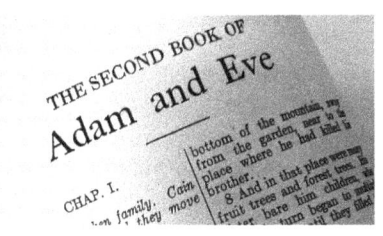 secular texts, among the library of books within the Dead Sea Scrolls, pseudepigraphic texts were also found. This should not be seen as acceptance of these works as canonical any more than the presence of religious novels in a store that sells Bibles would attest to their inspiration.

Old Testament Reliability

Can we trust the text of the Old Testament? Have the books of the Hebrew Bible come down to us as God revealed them to the Old Testament prophets? We have seen God's providence in revealing His written word at the earliest stages in the history of

How We Got the Bible

written language. We have seen God's preservation of His word in times of unfaithfulness and oppression. We have seen that the Old Testament we still have was known to Jesus and even those before His time. As a result we can be assured that the Old Testament Law, Prophets, and Writings (Genesis through Malachi) were complete and viewed as the inspired word of God well before the first century. We can be assured that the Old Testament we read in sound translations of our English Bibles is the complete, accurate, and wholly inspired word of God.

Discussion Questions

1. What are the two types of writing media mentioned in Scripture? On which of these have copies of Scripture been preserved?
2. What are some advantages of alphabetic writing?
3. What three major events influenced the development of the Old Testament?
4. What is the "Documentary Hypothesis" and what are some facts th at discredit it?
5. Is the phrase "books of the Law" ever found in Scripture? What does this indicate about what was brought to Josiah?
6. What are the three divisions of the Hebrew Bible? How do we know Jesus accepted these divisions?
7. What is the Septuagint? How has it influenced the Bible as we have it in English?
8. Why shouldn't the books of the Apocrypha be viewed as part of the biblical canon?

The Formation of the New Testament

In this portion of our study, we will consider what is known about the formation of New Testament. A study of this nature is forced, to some extent, to examine historical evidence in order to refute arguments that seek to discredit Scripture. Even so, we cannot emphasize enough that the value of Scripture comes from what it teaches us. The aim of our study is to bolster faith, to help overcome doubt, and to establish greater confidence in the Bible as the complete, inerrant, and wholly inspired word of God.

Language in the First Century

To begin this effort, we must, as we did in the first chapter, start with a consideration of the tools the Holy Spirit used to reveal Scripture.

Languages of the Bible. The Bible was written in three languages: *Hebrew* – For most of the Old Testament; *Aramaic* – In a few passages of the Old Testament and some words in the New Testament, and *Koine Greek* for most of the New Testament.

Aramaic (like Greek) became an international language during the period of the Persian empire. It was one of the spoken languages of Jews in the First Century. Jesus and His disciples spoke Aramaic and Greek. We

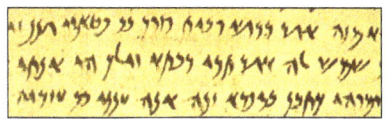

Ancient Aramaic

How We Got the Bible

see this in many words and phrases that are actually transliterated out of Aramaic into Greek. Such as the phrase *"Talitha cumi"* meaning *"Little girl, rise up"* (Mark 5:41). Or Jesus' words from the cross, *"Eli, Eli, lama sabachthani?"* Aramaic for *"My God, My God, why have You forsaken Me"* (Matt. 27:46). Other common words such as *abba, rabboni, mammon,* and *Cephas* are all Aramaic. Even so, the only New Testament manuscripts in Aramaic (or Syriac) are translations from the original Greek.

Koine (i.e. "Common") Greek became the new international language with the conquest of Alexander the Great. This brought the Greek language to much of the ancient world. The Septuagint (LXX) translation of the Old Testament done before Christ was the Old Testament for Greek speaking Jews and early Christians.

We noted in the previous chapter the fact that God's choice to reveal His word at the very beginning of man's use of alphabetic writing allowed the common man to have greater

Koine Greek

access to Scripture. We have come to understand exactly how the providence of God played into the utilization of Koine Greek as well. Dana and Mantey, in their *Manual Grammar of New Testament Greek*, wrote:

> There was a time when the scholars who dealt with the original text of the New Testament regarded its Greek as a special Holy Ghost language, prepared under divine direction for the Scripture writers.... [Now it is understood that]...New Testament Greek is simply a sample of the colloquial Greek of the first century.... The inspired writers... wrote in the ordinary language of the masses.... (9-10).

In the same way, that the Hebrew script underwent changes, the Greek script used in copying New Testament manuscripts went through similar transitions. This transition assists us in dating manuscripts. Early Greek was written in what was called *uncial* or *majuscule* script (i.e. upper case letters with all words connected together). This was used through AD 900. Over time Greek began, after about AD 800, to be written in *minuscule* script (i.e. lower case letters with words separated and with breathing and accent signs added to aid in pronunciation). This is the way modern Greek is written today and the way that most editions of the Greek New Testament are printed.

Writing Material. As in the Old Testament, a common writing media of ancient times was the scroll, written on either papyrus or parchment. New Testament times and beyond saw the rise of what is known as the *codex*. The codex was made of leaves (or pages) bound together with writing on both sides. We call this a "book." Some scholars think that the development of the codex itself came as a result of the move to copy Scripture and teach the gospel.

Ancient Codex

These were the tools the Holy Spirit used to reveal the New Covenant, a phase of God's dealings with mankind that was dependent upon a clear promise in the Old Testament...

The Coming of the Messiah

The Old Testament promised the coming of an individual who would be a king, a prophet, the Messiah (i.e. the "anointed one"), and God in the flesh. The Mosaic Law promised, *"The Lord your God will raise up for you a Prophet like me from your midst, from your brethren. Him you shall hear"* (Deut. 18:15). *"Therefore the Lord Himself will give you a sign: Behold the virgin shall conceive and bear a Son, and shall call His name Immanuel"* (Isa. 7:14). This name *Immanuel* was more than a personal name. It literally means "God with us." The prophet Daniel declared,

How We Got the Bible

"Know therefore and understand that from the going forth of the command to restore and build Jerusalem until Messiah the Prince, there shall be seven weeks and sixty-two weeks..." (Dan. 9:25).

Jesus of Nazareth, came forth as the promised Messiah. He claimed to be the Messiah. When Jesus talked with a Samaritan woman by the well, John records for us, *"The woman said to Him, 'I know that Messiah is coming (who is called Christ). When He comes, He will tell us all things.' Jesus said to her, 'I who speak to you am He'"* (John 4:25-26). He also accepts other people's claims that He is the Messiah. Jesus asked His disciples, *"'...Who do you say that I am?' And Simon Peter answered and said, 'You are the Christ, the Son of the Living God.' Jesus answered and said to Him, 'Blessed are you ...flesh and blood has not revealed this to you, but My Father who is in heaven'"* (Matt. 16:15-17). Jesus fulfilled prophecy pointing to the Messiah. There are scores of examples of this, but we notice a few that could not have been faked by an imposter:

- He was born in Bethlehem and taught in Galilee (Mic. 5:2; Isa. 9:1-2).
- He was of the tribe of Judah and a descendant of David (Gen. 49:10; Isa. 9:7).
- His side was pierced, yet He had no broken bones (Zech. 12:10; Ps. 34:20).
- He died with the wicked, but was buried with the rich (Isa. 53:9).

The Gospels

Jesus Himself produced no written texts. Yet, He commanded His disciples to go forth and teach. He issued what we call the "Great Commission." He said to His disciples, *"Go therefore and*

How We Got the Bible

make disciples of all the nations, baptizing them in the name of the Father and of the Son and of the Holy Spirit, teaching them to observe all things that I have commanded you..." (Matt. 28:19-20). He promised them that the Holy Spirit would come upon them and aid them in this effort. He said, *"However, when He, the Spirit of truth, has come, He will guide you into all truth...."* (John 16:13). *"...He will teach you all things, and bring to your remembrance all things that I said to you"* (John 14:26). As a result, the apostles could claim, as Paul did, *"...the things which I write to you are the commandments of the Lord"* (1 Cor. 14:37).

Some of the most important of these writings by Jesus' apostles and Christian prophets are the *Gospels*. These are the first four books of the New Testament that record the life of Jesus on the earth. The word *gospel* literally means "good news." These books were written by the apostles Matthew and John, and two early disciples—John Mark (a relative of Barnabas) and Luke a traveling companion of Paul on his preaching trips. We do not have the exact dates of when these texts were written. However, scholars look at internal and external evidence to roughly place Mark in the 60s; Matthew and Luke in the 70s; and John in the 80s. Some, including most ancient sources, put Matthew first, which would date it to somewhere in the 40s or 50s.

Ancient writers have some valuable comments on the writing of the Gospels. Irenaeus of Lyons (ca. AD 180) describes how the Gospels were written telling us:

> ...Matthew among the Hebrews issued a Writing of the gospel in their own tongue, while Peter and Paul were preaching the gospel at Rome and founding the church. After their decease Mark, the disciple and interpreter of Peter, also handed down to us in writing what Peter had preached. Then, Luke, the follower of Paul, recorded in a book the gospel as it was preached by him. Finally John, the disciple of

How We Got the Bible

the Lord... himself published the gospel while he was residing at Ephesus in Asia (*Against Heresies* 3.1).

Irenaeus did not view these writings as man-made texts. Speaking of Jesus' first disciples he says:

> They first preached it abroad and then later by the will of God handed it down to us in Writings, to be the foundation and pillar of our faith.... For after our Lord had risen from the dead, they were clothed with power from on high when the Holy Spirit came upon them, they were filled with all things and had perfect knowledge (*ibid*.)

Man Says This Isn't True! There have always been those who have tried to claim that the New Testament was not from God. In recent generations, this assault has clothed itself in the "scholarly" garb of B. H. Streeter's *Q* Hypothesis. This hypothesis draws its name from the German word *Quelle* meaning "source." It claims that there was a hypothetical document which was written before any of the Gospels that contained Jesus' sayings. This hypothesis claims that, where Matthew and Luke differ from Mark, *Q* was their source. According to the hypothesis, Luke supposedly follows the order of *Q* more closely than Matthew.

What is the truth about this theory? First, it must be recognized that simply because we find similar wording and arrangement does not show that texts share some common written sources. The works themselves offer the reason for their similarity in the fact that the Holy Spirit was their common source. Jesus promised, *"But the Helper, the Holy Spirit, whom the Father will send in my name, He will teach you all things, and bring to your remembrance all things that I said to you"* (John 14:26). Paul claimed, *"These things we also speak, not in words which man's wisdom teaches but which the Holy Spirit teaches..."* (1 Cor. 2:13).

How We Got the Bible

Further, early Christian writers do not speak of a *Q* source. We see this in the claims of three early writers who all claim that the Gospel writers wrote the Gospels themselves. Origen of Alexandria (ca. AD 210), in the introduction to his commentary on Matthew wrote, "I have learned by tradition that the Gospel according to Matthew, who was ... an Apostle of Jesus Christ, was written first;.... The second written was that according to Mark, who wrote it according to the instruction of Peter,... And third, was that according to Luke, the Gospel commended by Paul, ... Last of all, that according to John..." As noted earlier, Origen claimed that Matthew was written first, but says nothing of a *Q* source document. The same is true of Irenaeus of Lyons (ca. 180 AD), quoted above. He claimed the gospel writers penned the works themselves and does not speak of a *Q* source document.

The closest to any claim of a source document and some early text, to which advocates of this view often appeal, is a statement made by Papias of Hierapolis (ca. 120 AD). Papias only addresses the composition of Matthew and Mark, but says..."Matthew collected the oracles (Gr. *logia*) in the Hebrew language, and each interpreted them as best he could" (as quoted in Eusebius' *Ecclesiastical History,* Book Three, 39.16). Were these *logia* a *Q* source? Edgar J. Goodspeed, in his book *Matthew: Apostle and Evangelist* writes in reference to Papias' words:

> Papias' observation about Matthew's connection with The Sayings (*logia*), is naturally understood to mean taking down Jesus' words as he uttered them..... His further statement that each one translated them as best he could seems to refer primarily to the Twelve.... I cannot see that any published book of these sayings is indicated, as is often assumed (88).

The *Q* source theory seeks to discredit the Bible's clear claims of inspiration. While there are many disjointed fragments

How We Got the Bible

of biblical and non-biblical sayings attributed to Jesus that have been discovered, there is no evidence for this false theory.

The New Testament Canon

The Gospels are not the only inspired writings produced by the disciples of Christ. There are twenty-seven "books" that the Holy Spirit has preserved for us as the *constitution* of the New Covenant of Jesus Christ. These are comprised of:

Books of History. There are five books of history. The four Gospels, that record the life of Christ and one book addressing the Acts of the Apostles. This text records the history of the church. The gospel of Luke and the book of Acts are really *Volume One* and *Volume Two* of Luke's history of Christ and the early church.

Letters (or *Epistles*) to Churches. These texts are correspondence from Paul to various churches. They address problems, offer encouragement, and teaching that constitute further revelation of the gospel of Christ.

Letters (or *Epistles*) to Individuals. Like the epistles to churches these texts offer instruction and encouragement to preachers or individual Christians in need of exhortation.

General Epistles. These works are not directed to individuals or churches, but to believers in general. These are written by apostles and early disciples (two of whom were the Lord's brothers, James and Jude). Then finally...

One Book of Prophecy. While the book of Revelation is the only one book categorized as prophecy in the New Testament, properly, all revealed Scripture is *prophecy* in that it was revealed prophetically by the Holy Spirit to the inspired writer. Even so, prophetic writing is often distinguished from historical or

How We Got the Bible

instructional writing when it addresses predictive prophecy as opposed to instructional prophecy. The *Apocalypse,* or Revelation of John, revealed to the apostle John as he was exiled on the island of Patmos, warns early churches of coming persecution and God's deliverance of His people.

These books comprise the New Testament canon and were written from the time after Jesus ascended into heaven until near the end of the First Century.

The Early Church's Use of New Testament Books

A grave false doctrine that our world asserts (almost unchallenged) is that the books of the New Testament were not written by eye witnesses to the events described (let alone under the inspiration of the Holy Spirit), but centuries after these events. We must oppose this emphatically! It is a lie and contrary not only to the claims of Scripture itself, but to the evidence of history. Note some examples of this evidence…

Early church writers quote from the New Testament. The respected New Testament Greek scholar Bruce Metzger, in his book, *The Text of the New Testament,* observes, "Indeed, so extensive are these citations that if all other sources of our knowledge of the text of the New Testament were destroyed, they would be sufficient alone for the reconstruction of practically the entire New Testament" (86).

The New Testament was used in worship in the early church. Justin Martyr (ca. AD 150), in describing the Lord's Supper, states, "For the apostles, in the memoirs composed by them, which are called Gospels, thus handed down what was commanded them: that Jesus, taking bread and having given thanks said, 'Do this for my memorial, this is my body...'" (*First Apology* 66). In describing worship on the Lord's Day he says

How We Got the Bible

further, "And on the day that is called Sunday there is a meeting in one place of those who live in cities or the country, and the memoirs of the apostles or the writings of the apostles are read as long as time permits" (*First Apology* 67).

The New Testament was used as a source of authority in the early church. Clement of Rome (ca. AD 96) writing to the church in Corinth says, "Take up the epistle of the blessed Paul the Apostle. What he wrote to you in the beginning of the Gospel? Of a truth he charged you in Spirit concerning himself and Cephas and Apollos, because that even then ye had made parties" (*To the Corinthians* 47.1). Ignatius of Antioch (ca. AD 100) writing to the church in Philadelphia says, "...Taking refuge in the Gospel, as in Jesus' flesh, and in the apostles, as in the presbytery of the church. And the prophets,...because they anticipated the gospel in their preaching and hoped for and awaited Him..." (*To the Philadelphians* 5). Ignatius, who sadly very early reflects apostasy regarding a single bishop over a church, writing to the church in Philadelphia spoke of his critics as saying, "...If I don't find it in the original documents, I don't believe it is in the gospel" (*To the Philadelphians* 8).[1] Papias of Hierapolis (ca. AD 120) held in higher esteem those who had met and talked with the apostles, over New Testament writings. In speaking of his own habit of asking anyone who had known the apostles what they had said,

---

[1] Some understand the phrase in the text translated "original documents" to refer to the Old Testament Scriptures. Yet, just before this he contrasted *"The Gospel"* and *"The Apostles"* (i.e. the New Testament) with *"The Prophets"* (i.e. the Old Testament) (*ibid.* 6). The critic wouldn't look to the Old Testament for "The Gospel." He then goes on to describe Jesus, the cross, and His resurrection as "the inviolable archives." This reflects a conflict between relying upon oral versus written authority (cf. Papias views above), but nonetheless exemplifies the fact that the New Testament was already held as an authority, at least by some, in these early days.

How We Got the Bible

Papias says... "For I did not suppose that information from books would help me so much as the word of the living and surviving voice" (as quoted in Eusebius' *Ecclesiastical History,* Book Three, 39.16). The fact that he articulates this view very early, implies that many already valued the "information from books" (i.e. New Testament books).

Books after the New Testament

Many religious writings were produced in the period after the New Testament was completed. Two important groups of these writings are: *The Apostolic Fathers* and *Gnostic Writings*.

The Apostolic Fathers is a term applied to the earliest Christian writing after the New Testament. It draws its name from the fact that some of these authors knew the apostles. For instance, Polycarp knew the apostle John. The *Apostolic Fathers* include *1* and *2 Clement*, the *Epistle of Barnabas*, the epistles of Ignatius, the epistles of Polycarp, the so-called *Didache* (or "Teaching of the Twelve") and a work known as the *Shepherd of Hermas*. Some early New Testament manuscripts include some of these works as supplemental texts. These works offer insight into church history and apostasy, but were not considered inspired.

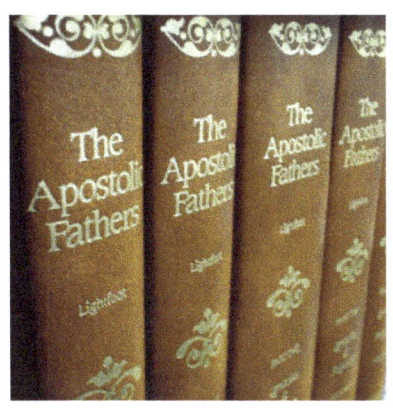

This is made clear by early writers. Tertullian of Carthage (ca. AD 200) critical of *The Shepherd's* allowance of forgiveness to adulterers, says that it, "... deserved to find a place in the Divine

How We Got the Bible

canon; if it had not been habitually judged by every council of Churches (even of your own) among apocryphal and false (writings); itself adulterous..." (*On Modesty* 10). Eusebius of Caesarea (ca. AD 320) claimed, "Among the rejected writings must be reckoned also the *Acts of Paul*, and the so-called *Shepherd*, and the *Apocalypse of Peter*, and in addition to these the extant *Epistle of Barnabas,* and the so-called Teachings of the Apostles..." (*Ecclesiastical History* 3.25). He wrote earlier in the same text, "...of Hermas, to whom the book called the *Shepherd* is ascribed, ... cannot be placed among the acknowledged books; while by others it is considered quite indispensable, especially to those who need instruction in the elements of the faith. Hence, as we know, it has been publicly read in churches, and I have found that some of the most ancient writers used it" (*Ecclesiastical History* 3.3). As we see in these statements, such works were esteemed, but not viewed as inspired, which stands them in clear contrast to how New Testament texts were viewed.

Gnostic Writings. The Bible makes it very clear that Jesus and the apostles warned that there would be "apostasy" (i.e. a turning away) from truth. Jesus said, *"Beware of false prophets, who come to you in sheep's clothing, but inwardly they are ravenous wolves"* (Matt. 7:15). Paul wrote, *"For the time will come when they will not endure sound doctrine, but according to their own desires, because they have itching ears, they will heap up for themselves teachers; and they will turn their ears away from the truth, and be turned aside to fables"* (2 Tim. 4:3, 4). The fact of apostasy does not change the truth of Scripture.

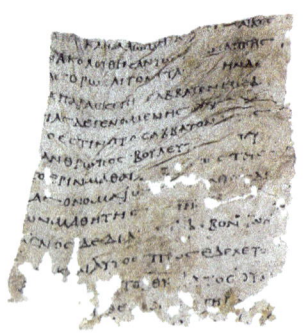

Tatian's Diatessaron

How We Got the Bible

There are many ways that apostasy manifested itself in the early church. As mentioned above, Ignatius, one of the "Apostolic Fathers," accepted a departure from the New Testament pattern in the organization of the church. He describes one bishop over one church. This small change ultimately led to the creation of the Roman Catholic church as it exists today. Yet, a blatant and most hideous apostasy that also developed very early came to be known as "Gnosticism."

Gnostic False Doctrines

Among some of the false doctrines associated with the various groups referred to as "Gnostics" was the belief that the God of the Old Testament was not the Father of Jesus, but a wicked God of warfare and evil. Some taught that Jesus did not actually come in the flesh but only appeared to come in the flesh. The Gnostics treated biblical villains such as Cain, Judas, and the Sodomites as heroes. Yet, they treated biblical heroes as villains. The Gnostics produced a significant number of heretical texts, including ...

The Gospel of Thomas

Tatian's Diatessaron. This work, was basically a harmony of the four Gospels, but it left out the genealogies of Jesus that showed His fleshly ancestry. This was widely used among Syriac churches for quite some time.

The Gospel of Thomas. A work that portrayed Jesus as saying... "Condemned be the flesh that depends upon the soul. Condemned be the soul that depends upon the flesh" (112). This reflects the Gnostic view that the flesh was corrupt by nature and thus man cannot avoid pursuing the desires of the flesh.

How We Got the Bible

The Gospel of Mary Magdalene. In this text Jesus, speaking like a Gnostic, says, "There is no sin. It is you who make sin exist, when you act according to the habits of your corrupted nature; this is where sin lies" (p. 7, lines 15-19).

The Gospel of Judas. A text only recently discovered, but known since the time of Irenaeus, treats Judas as the real hero of Jesus' earthly ministry. It has Jesus telling Judas, "But you will exceed all of them. For you will sacrifice the man that clothes me." Irenaeus (ca. 180 AD) in his work, *Against Heresies* wrote about the Gnostics and this text saying, "...They declare that Judas the traitor was thoroughly acquainted with these things, and that he alone, knowing the truth as no others did, accomplished the mystery of the betrayal; by him all things, both earthly and heavenly, were thus thrown into confusion. They produce a fictitious history of this kind, which they style the Gospel of Judas" (1.31.1).

The Gospel of Judas

Marcion's Heresy. Irenaeus also tells us about another Gnostic named Marcion. Marcion's work demonstrates the serious threat that gnosticism mounted against the text of Scripture itself. Irenaeus wrote that Marcion

> ...Mutilates the Gospel which is according to Luke, removing all that is written respecting the generation of the Lord, and setting aside a great deal of the teaching of the Lord, in which the Lord is recorded as most dearly confessing that the Maker of this universe is His Father.... In like manner, too, he dismembered the Epistles of Paul removing all that is said by the apostle respecting that God who made the world, to the effect that He is the Father of our Lord Jesus Christ, and also those passages from the prophetical writings which the Apostle quotes, in order to teach us that they announced beforehand the coming of the Lord. [Marcion] ...dared openly to mutilate Scriptures (*Against Heresies* 1.27.2, 4).

How We Got the Bible

This motivated many who rejected these heresies to move forcefully to oppose Gnostic writings and teachings. Some of the councils and "Canon lists" came about in response to some of these false doctrines.

Ecumenical Councils and Canon Lists

God never authorized "councils" of men to determine what was right or wrong. God never authorized published declarations of men to declare what was and was not true. Nonetheless, in response to many false doctrines man presumed to do exactly that. Councils, creeds, and declarations of man hold no authority. In some cases, however, they do give us insight into what people believed at a given point in history. Sometimes these records are nothing more than a man stating what he believed to be the case. Other times they reflect the arrogance of man, attempting to exert authority that man does not possess. Either way, it is a mistake to imagine that the fate of God's word or the definition of what is God's word was determined through some deliberative process of man. God revealed, God preserved, and God sustains His word.

Ancient Canon List

Canon Lists

There have been preserved a number of so-called "canon lists" that record what a particular writer, leader, or council understood to be the extent of the biblical canon. Canon lists do not reflect a human process of choosing what was or was not inspired. Canon lists are a reflection of personal or collective belief at a given time. Some show sound analysis of Scripture, others do not. This does not indicate anything about the veracity of Scripture, but simply the fact that man has freewill.

How We Got the Bible

What determines whether something is canonical? There are two ways I want to frame this question: What determines what *is* canonical and what determined what was *viewed* as canonical. One part of this addresses God's role while the other addresses the issues man looks at in determining what he will accept.

Divine Providence. We can never take too lightly the clear assertions in Scripture that God always preserves His word. Remember, Jesus declared, *"For assuredly, I say to you, till heaven and earth pass away, one jot or one tittle will by no means pass from the law till all is fulfilled"* (Matt. 5:18). This shows God's preservation of His word, and Jesus' belief that every "jot" and "tittle" was from God. He said, *"...All flesh is as grass, and all the glory of man as the flower of the grass. The grass withers, and its flower falls away, but the word of the LORD endures forever..."* (1 Pet. 1:24-25). God has not revealed His word only to allow the rebellion of man to wipe it out of existence. Yet, the next part of the question is...

What Determined What Was Viewed As Canonical? Basically it is clear that early religious leaders looked at a few criteria:

1. *Acceptance by the early church.* We noted above the mass of evidence among early religious writers that demonstrates what was viewed as inspired and what was not.

2. *Apostolic connection.* Was the work written by one of the apostles or those closely associated with them?

3. *Content.* The overt heretical teaching of Gnostic texts made it clear that they were the works of men. The use of human reasoning or misunderstanding bore witness to the same fact. In the work among the *Apostolic Fathers* known as the "Epistle of Barnabas," its writer cited the mythical bird called the Phoenix

How We Got the Bible

being reborn out of fire to illustrate the truth of the resurrection. The Latin scholar Jerome (ca. 342-420) once commented that intertestamental apocryphal texts were like "...the crazy wanderings of a man whose senses have taken leave of him" (*Epist.* 57.9). He did not believe that the Apocrypha was canonical. Such things made it clear when a text was of human origin.

Did Nicea Address the Canon? It is often asserted incorrectly that the New Testament canon was decided at the Council of Nicea. This Council was convened by the emperor Constantine, the first emperor who believed in Jesus. While this council did address the nature of Christ and opposition to Gnostic heresies, there is very little indication that they issued any statement about what was and what was not in the canon. In his preface to his translation of the apocryphal book of Judith, Jerome says, "Among the Jews, the book of Judith is considered among the Apocrypha; .... Moreover, since it was written in the Chaldean language, it is counted among the historical books. But the Nicene Council is considered to have counted this book among the number of sacred Scriptures...." This is the sole evidence that some look to in claiming that Nicea "determined" the Canon. All that this in fact indicates is that Jerome understood some at the council to have accepted this book. Anything more than that is supposition.

Emperor Constantine

Other council statements did address the extent of the Canon:

The Synod of Laodocia (343-381) Issued this statement, "... And these are the books of the New Testament: Four Gospels, according to Matthew, Mark, Luke and John; The Acts of the Apostles; Seven Catholic [i.e. "universal"] Epistles, to wit, one of James, two of

How We Got the Bible

Peter, three of John, one of Jude; Fourteen Epistles of Paul, one to the Romans, two to the Corinthians, one to the Galatians, one to the Ephesians, one to the Philippians, one to the Colossians, two to the Thessalonians, one to the Hebrews, two to Timothy, one to Titus, and one to Philemon" (Canon 60).

The Letter of Athanasius (367 AD) states: "...Of the New Testament. These are, the four Gospels, according to Matthew, Mark, Luke, and John. Afterwards, the Acts of the Apostles and Epistles (called Catholic), seven, viz. of James, one; of Peter, two; of John, three; after these, one of Jude. In addition, there are fourteen Epistles of Paul, written in this order. The first, to the Romans; then two to the Corinthians; after these, to the Galatians; next, to the Ephesians; then to the Philippians; then to the Colossians; after these, two to the Thessalonians, and that to the Hebrews; and again, two to Timothy; one to Titus; and lastly, that to Philemon. And besides, the Revelation of John" (Festal Letter 39).

After the letter of Athanasius, councils in Hippo (393 AD), Carthage (397 AD), and Rome in (405 AD) eventually acknowledged this same list. This should not be seen as these men and councils determining what was in Scripture, but simply stating what they understood to be the case.

Was Something Left Out? The question arises, *"Does the fact that some lists (and manuscripts) contain other texts mean that something may have been left out of modern Bibles?"* No! It simply reflects the fact that some valued those texts. Some may have viewed them as supplemental. Some may have mistakenly taken them as inspired. Councils or declarations of men do not determine what is Divine, inspired, or authoritative. At best, they simply state what was already understood to be true.

How We Got the Bible

New Testament Reliability

The New Testament Gospels, Epistles, and Prophecy (Matthew to Revelation) were complete and viewed as the inspired word of God by the end of the First Century. We can be assured that the New Testament we read in sound translations of our English Bible is (with the Old Testament) the complete, accurate, and wholly inspired word of God.

Discussion Questions

1. What three languages were utilized by the Holy Spirit to produce Scripture and where were they used?
2. What is meant by the term *Koine* Greek?
3. What is a *codex* and how does it differ from a scroll?
4. What are four prophecies confirmed in the life of Jesus that could not have been faked?
5. What do biblical theorists mean by the term *Q* and what are some answers to the false claims of this theory?
6. What are the five categories of books that comprise the New Testament and what books fall into these categories?
7. What does the fact that early church writers quote from the New Testament indicate about when it was written?
8. What are the texts called the *Apostolic Fathers* and how do they differ from Gnostic writings?
9. Did councils or canon lists determine what was or was not in Scripture? Why or why not?

The History of the English Bible

One of the most dramatic aspects of the entire question of how we got the Bible concerns how it was conveyed to men and women of different tongues. To this point in our study, we have looked at the formation of Scripture and the providence of God in bringing His word to man. We have refuted false theories that seek to undermine the inspiration and revelation of this word. If we stopped here, we might be led to imagine that, when revelation was completed, the next day there was an English Bible in every hotel night-stand, every home, every church, and all could read it freely. Nothing could be further from the truth.

In 1724, Isaac Watts wrote a song that is in many of our hymnbooks entitled, *Am I a Soldier of the Cross?* One line in this hymn asks the question, "Must I be carried to the skies on flow'ry beds of ease, while others fought to win the prize and sailed through bloody seas?" In the consideration of how the Bible came into the English language we will come to see, perhaps as never before, what a privilege it is to sit in comfortable pews, in warm buildings, without fear, without persecution, to hear preached, to see projected in high-tech computer projection, and to open the pages of our own, personal, easy to understand Bible. This privilege did not just happen. It was paid for with the blood, zeal, and lives of those who have gone before us.

How We Got the Bible

The Translation of the New Testament

The pouring out of the gift of tongues on the day of Pentecost demonstrated the challenge early Christians faced if they were to take the Gospel of Jesus Christ into all the world. Since the confusion of tongues at the tower of Babel, different men and nations have spoken a variety of different languages. When the age of miraculous gifts passed away, the need came very quickly for those of different tongues to have the word of God accessible to them in their own language.

Early Translations. This process began at once. Among the first translations of the New Testament were those done in...

1. *Syriac (ca. 200s)*. In the second and third centuries, the Bible was translated into Syriac, a dialect of Aramaic used in the region of Antioch. The most widely accepted version of the Syriac Bible is called the Peshitta, meaning "pure." It remains the standard Bible among Syriac churches.

Syriac Peshitta

2. *Coptic (ca. 200s)*. Also in the second and third centuries the Bible was translated into Coptic, the form of Egyptian in use in the early centuries after Christ. Coptic was written making use of the Greek alphabet with a few additional letters to accommodate Egyptian sounds. It may be that the development of Coptic itself was heavily influenced by Bible translators.

Gothic Bible

3. *Gothic (ca. 300s)*. Around 350, a man named Wulfilas, began to translate portions of the Bible into the Gothic language. This Germanic language, was spoken by the Goths of Dacia.

How We Got the Bible

In order to accomplish this Wulfilas had to invent an alphabet for Gothic in order to even make a translation. The surviving text of Wulfilas' Bible is the primary surviving example of this language.

4. *Old Latin (200s)*. In the second and third centuries as well, the Bible was translated into Latin. The Latin language was rapidly growing to be the language of the Roman empire. Early translations of the Bible into the tongue of Rome came onto the scene very quickly.

5. *Armenian (400s)*. In the fifth century a man named Mesrop invented alphabets for the Armenian and Georgian languages for the purpose of translating the Bible into these tongues. The scripts which Mesrop developed are the alphabets still in use in Armenia and Georgia.

Armenian Bible

6. *Ethiopic (500s)*. In the fourth century, the New Testament was translated into Ethiopic (or *Ge'ez*). Jewish proselytes had been in Ethiopia for some time. As a result, the Old Testament was translated into Ethiopic well before this. Editions of this Ethiopic text are still in use today in Ethiopia among those who speak Amharic.

Ethiopic Bible

7. *Slavonic (800s)*. In the 800s, Cyril and Methodius, two brothers, taught among the Slavs. In order to translate the Bible, they too had to invent an alphabet for their language, now known as "Old Church Slavonic." The alphabet used in modern Russian is called Cyrillic, after the name of its inventor—Cyril. It is ironic that the alphabet used to write the

How We Got the Bible

"Old Church" Slavonic Bible

Russian language, of the former atheistic Soviet Union, was first created to translate Scripture.

"Into All the World." Jesus charged His apostles to, *"Go into all the world and preach the gospel to every creature. He who believes and is baptized will be saved; but he who does not believe will be condemned"* (Mark 16:15-16). Paul acknowledged that without such an effort to go out and teach the lost, they cannot come to faith. He asked, *"How shall they call on Him in whom they have not believed? And how shall they believe in Him of whom they have not heard? And how shall they hear without a preacher?"* (Rom. 10:14). We are reminded of the work of Ezra, when it is said of his move to teach the people, *"So they read distinctly from the book of the Law of God; and they gave the sense, and helped them understand"* (Neh. 8:8). What a humbling thought it is to realize that Jesus was proclaimed, without smart phones, without the internet, without computers, without printing presses, without airplanes, or automobiles.

The Latin Vulgate

Among all of the early translations that were done, none would gain such widespread acceptance as that initiated by the Latin scholar Jerome (ca. 342-420). Jerome was trained as a boy in Greek and Latin classics and grammar. At one point in his life, he actually withdrew from society and studied Hebrew as a hermit in a cave for a time. Jerome found the texts of the Latin Bible of his day coarse, confusing, and unsatisfactory. Commenting on the confusing state of the Old Latin Bible texts, he once said, "There are almost as many forms of the text as there are copies" (*Praef. ad Evan.*). While in Constantinople, Jerome served as

How We Got the Bible

the secretary to Damasus, the Roman Catholic bishop of Rome. Damasus assigned him to work on a new Latin translation.

Jerome traveled to Palestine and compared different manuscripts. Jerome (with others) prepared the first critical Latin translation of the Bible in 405. It was written in *Vulgar* (i.e. "Common") Latin, for the common man. The Vulgate (as it was called) came to be viewed as the official "authorized version" of Western Europe for a thousand years.

Latin Vulgate Bible

We must understand that as good as the Latin Vulgate may have been, it was nonetheless a translation. The original biblical texts were in Hebrew and Greek. Ironically, although it was intended for the common man, this fact would be ignored in later years by the Catholic church. While it represented excellent scholarship, it was not flawless.

"Test All Things." Christians should have a constant willingness to test the soundness of those things that can affect us spiritually. Paul wrote, *"Test all things; hold fast what is good"* (1 Thess. 5:21). We do this in recognition of the possibility of apostasy. Paul warned, *"For the time will come when they will not endure sound doctrine, but according to their own desires because they have itching ears they will heap up for themselves teachers and they will turn their ears away from the truth and be turned aside to fables"* (1 Tim. 4:3-4). It is right to make certain that copies of texts are accurate. It is right to make certain that translations are accurate. This does not reflect a lack of trust in God or the

How We Got the Bible

inspiration of Scripture, but rather good stewardship of those things entrusted to us.

The Middle Ages

The term "Middle Ages" is a period used to refer to the period after the fall of Rome, when Europe floundered in a gloomy period of stagnation and despair. This was due to many factors. The barbarian invasions of Europe set back much cultural advancement. The loss of central authority left Europe under the control of feudal lords and knights until nations grew to power and independence. The Roman Catholic church's control of Europe and its attitudes toward science, investigation, and learning left many illiterate and ignorant.

The Bible in the Middle Ages. During this period, only the wealthy could afford Bibles. All copies of Scripture were made by a scribe, by hand, and were thus very expensive and time consuming to produce. The common man was not encouraged to read the Scriptures.

Bibles were so expensive that in some cases they were literally chained to pulpits. The first Bible that the monk, Martin Luther ever saw was chained to a library wall. During this period, however, Scripture was *chained* in many ways. Although Latin was no longer the language of the common man, preaching was still done in Latin. Latin had become the language of Europe's scholars and the Latin Vulgate was the only Bible  accepted by the Catholic church who dominated Western Europe. The common people were largely ignorant of God's word. This period is rightly called the "Dark Ages."

How We Got the Bible

This period reminds us of other times and another people with the same problems. They suffered from...

Lack of Knowledge. In the days of Hosea the Lord said, *"My people are destroyed for lack of knowledge. Because you have rejected knowledge, I also will reject you from being priest for Me; Because you have forgotten the law of your God, I also will forget your children"* (Hos. 4:6). This was true because of the...

Shutting Off of the Word. Jesus rebuked the Pharisees, saying, *"But woe to you, scribes and Pharisees, hypocrites! For you shut up the kingdom of heaven against men; for you neither go in yourselves, nor do you allow those who are entering to go in"* (Matt. 23:13). This would end with ...

The Renaissance and the Reformation.

There were great things that resulted from the historical periods known as the *Renaissance* and the *Reformation*. While we would not embrace all that has resulted from these times, there is little question that during these years there were a number of things that changed history. Three of the most notable were: 1) The invention of the printing press; 2) The movement known as "Christian Humanism," and 3) The Protestant Reformation.

The Printing Press

At the close of the European Middle Ages parchment (animal skins tanned as a writing material) was still in use, but very expensive. Papyrus could only be imported from Egypt. Although papermaking was invented in China in the year AD 105, it did not make its way to Europe until 950. The first paper

Early Paper Making

How We Got the Bible

mill was set up in Spain in the year 1150. This made book making easier and cheaper.

With paper as a more accessible type of media, all that remained was a technique that could expedite producing texts themselves. In 1452, Johannes Gutenberg succeeded in operating the first printing press with moveable type. The first printed publication

Printing Press

was a papal indulgence, claiming to grant forgiveness of sins to the bearer. Yet, the most noteworthy text Gutenberg produced was the "42 Line" Bible. In 1457, Gutenberg began printing an edition of the Latin Vulgate named for its 42 lines per page. Typesetters took an entire day to layout one page of text. Even so, this allowed multiple copies to be rapidly produced at a rate much faster and less expensive than texts copied by hand.

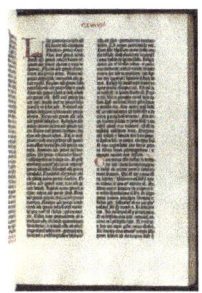

"42 Line" Bible

"Christian" Humanism. The term humanism in modern times is strictly focused on man. From the fourteenth through the sixteenth centuries, however, a movement spread across Europe known as *Humanism*. Unlike modern humanism that sees man as the focus of all things, "Christian" humanism fostered an appreciation for what man could do with the abilities God had given to him. This movement led to an appreciation of classical learning and the study of ancient Greek and Latin texts. This also engendered a strong desire to look back to original sources to test the veracity of texts. This movement became very significant to the history of the biblical text and to some individuals who embraced the humanist philosophy. Two of these notable figures were:

How We Got the Bible

Desiderius Erasmus. In 1504 a scholar named Desiderius Erasmus read a work by Lorenzo Valla entitled *Annotations on the New Testament*. Valla sought to look back to the original language of Scripture to overcome false concepts that had arisen over time. Erasmus was intrigued and set himself to the task of comparing manuscripts of the Greek New Testament to analyze the text. In 1516

Desiderius Erasmus

Erasmus published the first critical edition of the Greek New Testament with the Vulgate in a parallel column. In 1518 he replaced the Vulgate with his own translation. In the preface to his 1516 edition of the Greek New Testament Erasmus wrote:

Erasmus' Greek NT

I wish that the Scriptures might be translated into all languages so that not only the Scot and the Irish, but also the Turk and the Saracen might read and understand them. Then I long that the farm-laborer might sing them as he follows the plough, the weaver hum them to tune of his shuttle, the traveler beguile the weariness of the journey with their stories.

Erasmus was a professor of Greek at Cambridge for a number of years and influenced scores of other students of the Bible.

Robert Stephanus. In 1550 Robert Estienne (Latinized as Stephanus) published a revision in Geneva of Erasmus' text making use of more manuscripts than were available to Erasmus. Stephanus setup the chapter and verse divisions in use today. Stephanus' work came to be known as the "Text received by all" or *Textus*

Stephanus' Greek NT

How We Got the Bible

Receptus. These developments were influential upon a final and world changing development...

The Protestant Reformation

In 1517 a German monk named Martin Luther challenged the Catholic church's practice of selling indulgences. Although originally interested only in reforming Catholicism, Luther's ideas spawned a movement throughout Europe that rejected the authority of Rome.

Martin Luther

Luther's Bible. A motto of this reformation was *sola scriptura "the Scriptures alone."* In 1522, using Erasmus' Greek New Testament Luther made the first translation of the New Testament in German from the original Greek. This became the Bible of many Protestants and fueled the desire of other reformers to possess the Bible in their own tongue. Commenting on the nature of the Bible, Luther wrote,

Luther's Bible

> No clearer Book has been written in this wide world than the Holy Scriptures. Compared with all other books it is like the sun over all other lights. Don't let them lead you out of and away from it, much as they may try to do so. For if you step out, you are lost; they take you wherever they wish. If you remain within, you will be victorious.

The Bible is Sufficient. Although we must reject some of the conclusions Luther would later draw from Scripture, we wholeheartedly agree with his assessment of the value of Scripture. Paul told Timothy, *"All Scripture is given by inspiration of God, and is profitable for doctrine, for reproof, for correction, for instruction in righteousness, that the man*

How We Got the Bible

of God may be complete, thoroughly equipped for every good work" (2 Tim. 3:16, 17). Just before this, he praised Timothy declaring, *"From childhood you have known the Holy Scriptures, which are able to make you wise unto salvation through faith which is in Christ Jesus"* (2 Tim. 3:15). Man needs no priest to interpret them, council to define them, additional revelation to understand them, or great intellect to comprehend them. The Bible was given so that man can read, understand, and follow the word of God for himself. Paul wrote, *"When you read, you may understand my knowledge in the mystery of Christ"* (Eph. 3:4). This desire to look back to the Bible is perhaps one of the greatest legacies that the Reformation left behind.

The Bible into English

The beginning of the process that led to an English Bible began in the Middle Ages. In 735, Aldhelm and Bede translated the gospel of John into Anglo-Saxon, an ancient form of English. Later, in the 800s, King Alfred distributed Exodus, Psalms, and Acts to the people in Anglo-Saxon. Unfortunately no manuscripts of these works have survived, but simply the record of their existence. In 950, a priest named Aldred wrote Anglo-Saxon translations above the Latin text of an older manuscript of the gospels originally produced at Lindisfarne. These are known as the "Lindisfarne Gospels."

Lindisfarne Gospels

The Wycliffe Bible. The first Bible actually written in English was that which was produced under the influence of John Wycliffe. Wycliffe led a group of priests who believed that preaching should be done in the language of the people, not in Latin. These were later sarcastically called *Lollards* meaning "mutterers." He

How We Got the Bible

John Wycliffe

died in 1384. In 1395 one of Wycliffe's followers published the first entire translation of the Bible in English, translating it from Latin texts. Although this was a monumental effort to bring Scripture to the people, it was only a translation of a translation.

In 1408 the Lollards were outlawed. In 1428 pope Martin V ordered Wycliffe's body to be exhumed, burned, and his ashes scattered over a stream near his house. Nevertheless, the process of bringing the word of God into English had already begun and it would not be turned back.

Wycliffe Bible

The British Throne. We cannot understand how the Bible came into English without having a picture in mind of the kings and queens of England who affected how and when this would happen. Unlike our own time, in which political leaders have no influence over a citizens's personal faith, in sixteenth century Europe the throne held great influence on the practice of faith.

Kings and Queens of England
- Henry VIII (1509-1547).
- Edward VI (1547-1553).
- Mary I (1553-1558).
- Elizabeth I (1558-1603).
- James I (1603-1625).

We will examine how these rulers influenced the effort to bring the Bible into English. We will do so considering the texts that were produced during their reigns.

How We Got the Bible

The Tyndale Bible (1526)

William Tyndale came to Cambridge shortly after Erasmus left. He was very interested in Erasmus' writings and became skilled in Greek. In response to laws forbidding the translation of the Bible into English, William Tyndale went to Germany, where he translated the New Testament into English from the Greek. To one who was critical of his plan to translate the Bible into English, Tyndale once said, "If God spare my life, ere many years pass, I will cause a boy that driveth the plough shall know more of Scriptures than thou dost."

William Tyndale

Tyndale's New Testament was published in 1526 and smuggled into England. Editions of the Tyndale Bible became very popular among the common people. But, officials burned all copies they could find. In 1536, he was arrested, strangled, and burned at the stake. His dying words were, "Lord, open the king of England's eyes."

Tyndale Bible

The Tyndale Bible introduced many words into English for which he could find no existing word (e.g. *long-suffering*). The Tyndale Bible was more literal in some passages than some versions that followed it. For example, 1 Timothy 3:15 reads, *"But and yf I tarie longe, that then thou mayst yet have knowledge how thou oughtest to behave thyselfe in the housse of God, which is the congrecacion of the livinge God, the pillar and grounde of the trueth."* We note the archaic spellings used in Old English, but the meaning is clear.

How We Got the Bible

The Coverdale Bible (1535)
Tyndale was not able to complete a translation of the Old Testament. This task was left to those who would follow him. Miles Coverdale, worked in Germany with Tyndale and supported Luther's reforms. In 1535 he published a complete translation of the entire Bible into English. Unfortunately, he had to use Latin and German texts for the Old Testament. So, like the Wycliffe Bible, it was a translation of a translation.

Miles Coverdale

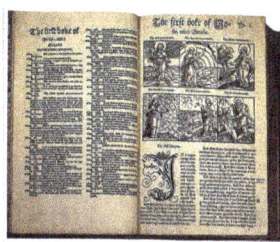
Coverdale Bible

The Matthew's Bible (1537)
In 1537, another friend of Tyndale, John Rogers, published another complete Bible, making use of some of Tyndale's unpublished notes. Rogers gave credit for the work to Thomas Matthew, but he is believed to have done most of the translation. Once again, however, the Old Testament was not done from Hebrew texts.

Matthew's Bible

The Great Bible (1539)
In the same year the Matthew's Bible was published, Miles Coverdale was commissioned by Thomas Cromwell, the chancellor of England to revise the Matthew's Bible. The so-called "Great Bible" was published in 1539 with the sanction of Henry VIII and used Hebrew texts to translate the Old Testament.

How We Got the Bible

Thomas Cromwell and Thomas Cranmer

Thomas Cromwell, Henry VIII's chancellor, did a great deal to move the crown towards allowing an English Bible. He was pictured to the left of the King on the title page of the Great Bible. Sadly, in 1540 he fell out of favor with the king and was executed by Henry VIII.

Thomas Cromwell

Thomas Cranmer

Thomas Cranmer, the Archbishop of Canterbury during the reign of Henry VIII, also did a great deal to move the crown towards allowing an English Bible. He was pictured to the right of the King on the title page of the Great Bible. He was burned at the stake in 1556 by the Catholic Queen Mary I.

Cover Page of the "Great Bible"
Thomas Cromwell (right), Henry VIII (center), Thomas Cranmer (left)

How We Got the Bible

The Council of Trent

In response to the rise of Protestantism a Council of Catholic theologians declared on April 8, 1546, that the Vulgate was the sole authoritative text in matters of faith and morals. The council acknowledged that the Vulgate was not without its imperfections and called for new revisions and corrections. The final revision of Pope Clement VIII, published in 1592, is known as the "Clementine Vulgate."

Council of Trent

Mary I – "Bloody Mary"

When Mary I came to the throne in 1553 many of the efforts towards freedom of worship and translation of the Bible into English were reversed. A strict Catholic, Mary Tudor persecuted Puritans and other Protestants. Public reading of the Bible in English was outlawed. Thomas Cranmer and John Rogers, the translator of the Matthews Bible, were burned at the stake. Miles Coverdale barely escaped from her with his life.

Mary I

The Geneva Bible (1557)

In response to the Queen's repression, many persecuted Puritans fled to Geneva. There in 1557, William Whittingham, John Calvin's brother-in-law, produced a revision of the Great Bible including Calvin's notes in the margins. This was the "Pilgrim's Bible" used by Puritan immigrants to America.

Its notes were largely produced by John Calvin and reflected his theological tenets. Calvin's notes on Romans 5:12 read:

How We Got the Bible

Text: 5:12 Wherefore, as by one man sin entered into the world, and death by sin; and so death passed upon all men, for that all have sinned:

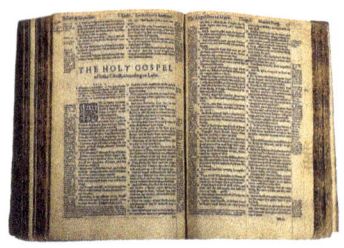

The Geneva Bible

Commentary: "From Adam, in whom all have sinned, both guiltiness and death (which is the punishment of the guiltiness) came upon all.... By sin is meant that disease which is ours by inheritance, and men commonly call it original sin.... ('all have sinned') That is, in Adam."

This reflected Calvin's false understanding of total hereditary depravity. The Bible teaches that sin can not be and is not inherited (Ezek. 18:20).

The Bishops' Bible (1568)

In 1568, Elizabeth I, unhappy with the Calvinistic notes of the Geneva Bible, assigned Matthew Parker to revise the Great Bible. Parker worked with eight Bishops and produced the "Bishops' Bible," to be placed in every church.

Rheims-Douay Bible (1582)

By the late 1500s, Rome finally accepted that an English Bible was inevitable. As a result, in 1582 Gregory Martin published an English New Testament for Catholics from the Latin Vulgate in Rheims. The Old Testament was published in 1609 from Douay. The *Rheims-Douay Bible* became the only English Bible authorized by the Catholic Church for generations. Having used the Latin Vulgate as its textual basis, it was another translation of a translation.

How We Got the Bible

The King James Version (1611)

King James I, in keeping with an agreement he made with Puritan leaders, assigned forty-seven scholars to create an "Authorized Version." Scholars from Oxford, Cambridge, and Westminster worked in six groups, who compared and checked one another's work. In 1611 (after seven years), it was published being the first English version with no doctrinal notes.

King James I

1611 King James Version

It is estimated that the "King James Version" followed 80-90% of Tyndale's text. In 1873 the Church of England issued a revision of the text, which is the text that is still called the *King James Version.*

The Look Changes but the Meaning Remains the Same. These dramatic events over the centuries have led to the privilege we now enjoy of being able to read the Bible in our own language. This privilege was purchased with blood and conviction. In spite of all the struggles, opposition, and different translations that came out of this period, there was in fact, a remarkable degree of consistency. Consider an example from Acts 2:38:

> **Tyndale Bible (1535):** "Peter sayde unto them: repent and be baptised every one of you in the name of Jesus Christ for the remission of synnes…" (Acts 2:38).
>
> **Great Bible (1540):** "Peter sayde unto them: repent of youre synnes, and be baptysed every one of you in the name of Jesus Christ for the remission of synnes…" (Acts 2:38).

How We Got the Bible

Geneva Bible (1562): "Then Peter sayd unto them, Amende your lyves, and be baptized everie one of you in the Name of Jesus Christ for the remission of sinnes…" (Acts 2:38).

Bishops' Bible (1602): "Then Peter sayd unto them, Repent ye, and let every one of you be baptized in the name of Jesus Christ for the remission of sinnes…" (Acts 2:38).

King James Version (1611): "Then Peter said unto them, Repent, and be baptized every one of you in the name of Jesus Christ for the remission of sins…" (Acts 2:38).

Did the rise of these various translations compromise the reliability of the text? Absolutely not! While not all translations are of the same quality, in the case of these early texts that opened the door to the word of God in English, the look of the text, may have changed, but the meaning remains ever the same.

Discussion Questions

1. What were the four earliest translations of the New Testament?
2. Who was responsible for the Latin Vulgate and what impact did it have on the ancient world?
3. Why were Bibles chained down in the Middle Ages?
4. How did the printing press and humanism influence the translation of the Bible into English?
5. Who translated the first New Testament into English from the Greek? What happened to him?
6. Who made widespread use of the *Geneva Bible*?
7. What was unique about the *King James Version* compared to other English translations before it?

Manuscript Discoveries and Modern Translations

We have seen God's wonderful hand in bringing about the formation of the Old Testament through the efforts of men and women of different backgrounds and experiences. Even so, the Old Testament forms a foundation for the hope that would come in Jesus Christ—the Messiah promised ages ago. We have seen the wonder of the New Testament—revealing in the face of persecution, heresy, and human weakness the power of God unto salvation. As those who speak a language much different from the language of the Bible, we have grown to appreciate all that has been done so that we can read the text in our own language and understand it. We have one last element to consider in order to bring our study to an end.

It is not uncommon to sit in a Bible class and hear the question, *"Why does my Bible say something different?"* An example of this is seen in Romans 8:1. The *New King James Version* reads:

> There is therefore now no condemnation to those who are in Christ Jesus, who do not walk according to the flesh, but according to the Spirit (Rom. 8:1, NKJV).

Yet, the *New American Standard Bible* reads simply:

> There is therefore now no condemnation for those who are in Christ Jesus (Rom. 8:1, NASB).

We have asserted in the previous chapters a confidence in the inspiration of Scripture as well as an assurance that God preserves His word. Yet, why do some versions differ?

How We Got the Bible

Reasons Versions Differ

There are several answers to this question:

1. The Style of Translation. Translators must decide what approach they will take in translation. They may choose a *literal* approach, in which as much as possible there is a "word for word" correspondence with the original language. They may take a *dynamic equivalence* approach. In this technique, the translator seeks to bring out the meaning of the passage when a "word for word" correspondence with the original language cannot be maintained. Or, the translator may choose to make a *paraphrase*. A paraphrase is not bound to the exact wording of a text, but summarizes the meaning. Whenever a translator moves beyond the exact wording, great caution must be exercised to avoid bias, and error. (See "Appendix: Choosing a Translation," 82).

2. Changes in Language. All languages change over time. Some translations differ as a result of such changes. A newer translation may seek to replace archaic forms with modern wording.

3. Different Textual Basis. Do Old Testament translators use the Masoretic Hebrew text as their basis or do they utilize discoveries from the Dead Sea Scrolls? Do New Testament translators rely on the Greek *Textus Receptus* or do they use "critical texts" that utilize modern discoveries?

These first two issues are addressed in the appendix. We will end our consideration of how we got the Bible with a consideration of the third reason that versions differ—the textual basis used for different translations.

The Textual Basis of a Translation

When we speak of the *textual basis*, we are considering what *text* the translator used in translating Scripture. Since we

How We Got the Bible

have no original manuscript, we must use editions that men have compiled based upon the study of manuscript copies of the Scriptures. While we contend that God in His providence preserves His word, this providence does not intervene to totally eliminate human mistakes in copying something. As a result, man must be diligent to test the accuracy of other men's efforts.

What Text Does the Translator Use? The question of what textual basis a translator uses depends upon which portion of the Bible he is considering. If the translators are working with Old Testament texts, they must choose between the traditional Hebrew text known as the Masoretic Text or critical texts making use of modern discoveries. If the translators are working on the New Testament, they must choose either the traditional Greek text known as the *Textus Receptus* or critical texts making use of modern discoveries.

We might ask, *what difference does it make?* In general, the differences are very minor. Compared to other written works, the very few differences that exist among different editions of the Hebrew or Greek Bible are quite minor indeed. Yet, there are a few differences. For example, consider a difference when it comes to Ephesians 5:9. One textual basis would read:

> For the fruit of the **Spirit** is in all goodness, righteousness and truth (Eph. 5:9, NKJV, emphasis mine).

Whereas, another textual basis reads:

> For the fruit of the **light** consists in all goodness and righteousness and truth (Eph. 5:9, NASB, emphasis mine).

Let's consider what accounts for these differences and on what basis we can make informed judgments.

How We Got the Bible

The Hebrew Masoretic Text

The Masoretes were Jewish scribes (ca. 500-1000) in Tiberias, Babylon, and Jerusalem who followed the *masorah* "tradition" of copying and preserving the Hebrew Old Testament.

The Masoretes developed the system of vowel markings used in Hebrew which aids in proper pronunciation. Originally, Hebrew was written without vowel markings. This is not as unusual as it may sound. Semitic languages lend themselves readily to being able to function with the vowels understood, without being written out. Many modern Hebrew texts still omit vowel markings. It would not be until around AD 500 that vowel markings would be developed to preserve proper pronunciation when Hebrew was no longer a commonly spoken language.

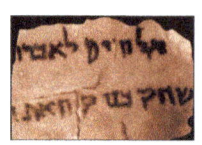
Without Vowels

With Vowels

The Masoretes carefully counted every letter of the text of the Hebrew Bible in order to preserve accuracy. They followed the practice of destroying damaged texts to prevent corruption of the text. While this did, in fact, preserve the veracity of the text, sadly it left few ancient copies that were preserved. One of the most important families among the Masoretes was that of Aaron ben Asher. The Hebrew text transmitted by the Masoretes is called the *Masoretic Text.*

Oldest Masoretic Texts

There are two primary examples of the Masoretic Text that have survived: the Aleppo Codex and the Leningrad Codex.

How We Got the Bible

Aleppo Codex

The Aleppo Codex was copied around 920 by Shlomo ben Buya'a and was verified by Aaron ben Asher. This text was used by the famous physician, philosopher, and theologian Maimonides. The Aleppo text was complete until 1947 when portions of it were lost in fire and riots.

The Leningrad Codex was copied in 1008 from manuscripts done by Aaron ben Asher. It is the oldest complete Masoretic Text. It is housed in St. Petersburg (formerly called Leningrad) in the Imperial Library.

Old Testament Time Gaps

With the Aleppo and Leningrad codices as the primary witnesses to the Hebrew text a 1300 year time gap was left from the time that the last book of the Old Testament was written to the earliest manuscript copy. Man asks the question, "Can we be confident that the text of the Old Testament we have today represents the Old Testament as it was originally written?"

God declared through Isaiah, *"So shall My word be that goes forth from My mouth; it shall not return to Me void, but it shall accomplish what I please, and it shall prosper in the thing for which I sent it"* (Isa. 55:11). The God who sends His word forth to accomplish His desire, will not allow His word to be lost forever. His providence has played a role in the preservation of Scripture and continues to do so.

Textus Receptus

We noted in the previous chapter the work of Desiderius Erasmus. In 1516, Erasmus published the first critical edition of the Greek New Testament reflecting his appreciation of

How We Got the Bible

humanist scholarship and a desire to look to the earliest sources to verify texts. His work was followed by Robert Stephanus (the Latinized name of Robert Estienne). In 1550, Stephanus published a revision in Geneva of Erasmus' text making use of more manuscripts. Stephanus' work came to be known as the "Text received by all" or *Textus Receptus.* There were additional editions which came out after this that are equally called the *Textus Receptus.* Of note were editions by Elziver and Scrivner.

This designation, *Textus Receptus* (or "Received Text") should not be misunderstood to mean that it was the "received text" in the sense that it was *received* from God in this form. Rather, it was the edition that gained general acceptance and reception by believers. It did, however, reflect the standard accepted text used in the Greek speaking world for generations.

It is clear that Erasmus and Stephanus had limited access to Greek manuscripts, yet, the texts they published represent what is found in the majority of the extant Greek manuscripts. Norman Geisler and Peter Bocchino, in their text *Unshakable Foundations,* identify 5686 Greek manuscripts of the New Testament (Minneapolis, MN: Bethany House Publishers, 2001, 256). If we add in ancient translations it brings the number to over 12,000 manuscripts.

New Testament Time Gaps. The publication of Erasmus' text left a 1400 years time gap between the accepted Greek text of the time and the date the last book of the New Testament was written. This leads man to ask again, "Can we be confident that the text of the New Testament we have today represents the New Testament as it was originally written?"

How We Got the Bible

We must reaffirm our absolute confidence in the providence of God. God revealed to Daniel that when the Roman empire would rule, *"in the days of these kings the God of heaven will set up a kingdom which shall never be destroyed and the kingdom shall not be left to other people; it shall break in pieces and consume all these kingdoms and it shall stand forever"* (Dan. 2:44). The God who promised to set up this eternal kingdom, will not allow His word to be lost forever! The providence of God has played a role throughout all ages in the preservation of Scripture.

Classification of Manuscripts

The renewed appreciation for the authority of the Bible, that came from the rise of "Christian Humanism" and the Protestant Reformation, led to a zealous interest in preserving and classifying Biblical manuscripts. We observed in previous chapters that the Greek language was originally written in *uncial* or *majuscule* script using all upper case letters with no breathings or space between words. This continued through about AD 900. After AD 800, Greek began to be written in *minuscule* script with mostly lower case letters, space between letters, and accent and breathing marks. While no difference in meaning resulted from this development, it allows scholars to identify the age of a manuscript based upon the style of the script used. In general terms *uncial* or *majuscule* manuscripts are older while *minuscule* manuscripts are younger. The renewed interest in looking back to the original language of Scripture led to the classification of three major *uncial* or *majuscule* manuscripts:

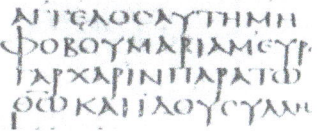
Uncial Script

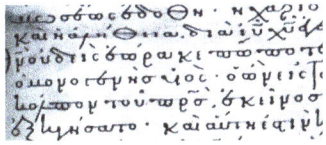
Minuscule Script

How We Got the Bible

Codex Alexandrinus

1. Codex Alexandrinus (A)
Sixteen years after the *King James Version* was published Cyril Lucar, Patriarch of Constantinople presented Charles I with a near complete Greek manuscript of the Bible believed to have come from Alexandria dating to around 400.

2. Codex Vaticanus (B)
Since at least 1475, in the earliest catalog of the Vatican library, there has been a near complete manuscript of the Greek Bible believed to date to about 300.

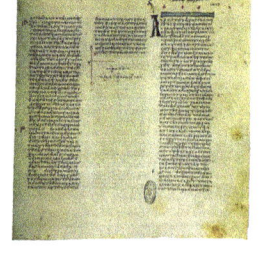
Codex Vaticanus

3. Codex Bezae (D)
Theodore Beza was a friend and successor of John Calvin. Beza was a scholar and developed the custom of italicizing words supplied by translators. In 1581, Beza gave Cambridge Library a manuscript of the Gospels and Acts that he had acquired from a monastery in Lyons dating to the fifth or sixth century.

Codex Bezae

The existence of each of these texts affirmed the wonderful degree to which God had preserved His word. As Jesus said, *"Heaven and earth will pass away, but My words will by no means pass away"* (Matt. 24:35). In spite of this, the nineteenth century would bring to light one of the most remarkable discoveries of the last two centuries…

How We Got the Bible

Codex Sinaiticus

The story of one of the most significant manuscript discoveries of modern times revolves around the life of a man named Constantin Tischendorf (1815-1874). Tischendorf was a child prodigy. At the age of nineteen, he was already a gifted scholar in Greek and Latin classics. At twenty-five, he was a university lecturer. At the age of twenty-six, he succeeded in the decipherment of the *palimpsest* (i.e. "scraped twice") manuscript, known as Codex Ephraemi. This manuscript, Codex Ephraemi Rescriptus (C) turned out to be a near complete manuscript of the New Testament from around AD 400. It was originally written on parchment, then scraped off some time later so that a work by a Syrian teacher named Ephraem could be written instead. While the original could be faintly seen underneath, no one until Tischendorf could visually filter out the earlier text from what was written on top of it. Tischendorf did just that!

Constantin Tischendorf

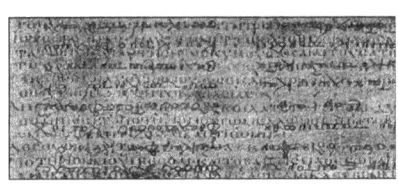
Codex Ephraemi Rescriptus

At twenty-seven, he published his first edition of the Greek New Testament. Two years later, in 1844 at the age of twenty-nine, he discovered the oldest complete New Testament manuscript ever known. While traveling to St. Catherine's monastery in the Sinai, Tischendorf rescued this ancient text before it was burned for firewood.

How We Got the Bible

Codex Sinaiticus (א)

Codex Sinaiticus dates to ca. AD 300 and was elegantly written in four columns on fine parchment. When collated back together it was found to contain all of the New Testament and much of the Greek Old Testament (LXX). Not only was Sinaiticus the oldest complete New Testament manuscript, but it was found to contain some twelve thousand variants from the *Textus Receptus*.

Codex Sinaiticus

One variant concerns the example we cited at the beginning of this chapter—Romans 8:1. While the majority of extant Greek manuscripts have the longer reading, Sinaiticus stopped with the words, *"There is therefore now no condemnation for those who are in Christ Jesus."* The text did have, however, a break in the line after the words for "Christ Jesus" with an arrow pointing back to these words. At the top of the page was a matching arrow with the words of the longer reading supplied (possibly) by a later editor.

Romans 8:1 from Sinaiticus

Another notable variant was found in the end of the gospel of Mark. Sinaiticus omitted 16:9-20, but left a large blank where the passage should have been. Many of the books of Sinaiticus have gaps like this, so it may not mean that the scribe knew it belonged there, but it is interesting. There are second century

Ending of Mark from Sinaiticus

How We Got the Bible

writers who quote the long reading, so we know that it was very ancient.[2]

Codex Sinaiticus served as the basis for Tischendorf's future editions of the Greek New Testament. He published a total of eight from 1841-1869. He once wrote:

Constantin Tischendorf

> No single work of ancient Greek classical literature can command three such original witnesses as the Sinaitic, Vatican, and Alexandrine Manuscripts, to the integrity and accuracy of its text. (*Introduction to the Authorized Version of the English New Testament* Lepzig, Winter 1868).

Three Witnesses

These three uncial manuscripts – Codex Sinaiticus (א), Codex Alexandrinus (A), and Codex Vaticanus (B), are viewed by some scholars as solid and incontrovertible witnesses to the original New Testament text. There is no question that these three uncial manuscripts provide remarkable witness to the New Testament text. In contrast to other ancient manuscripts the evidence for the text of the New Testament is remarkable (as seen from the chart on the next page). Yet, a number of questions arise. *Does the age of a manuscript guarantee its accuracy? Does a well preserved manuscript guarantee that it is accurate, or does it suggest that the manuscript fell into disuse for some reason? Should accepted readings be rejected based on the witness of a few manuscripts?* The way that scholars have answered these questions has led to two different approaches towards textual criticism: the *Critical Text Approach* and the *"Majority Text" Approach.*

---

[2] See my article, "Is Mark 16:9-20 Inspired?" *Biblical Insights* 9.8 (August 2009): 22-23, for more information.

How We Got the Bible

Manuscript Evidence for Ancient Texts

Author	Date Written Written	Earliest Copy	Time Span	Number of Copies
Plato	427-347 BC	AD 900	1200 yrs	7
Herodotus	480-425 BC	AD 900	1300 yrs	8
Thucydides	460-400 BC	AD 900	1300 yrs	8
Euripides	480-406 BC	AD 1100	1300 yrs	9
Caesar	100-44 BC	AD 900	1000	10
Tacitus	circa AD 100	AD 1100	1000 yrs	20
Aristotle	384-322 BC	AD 1100	1400 yrs	49
Sophocles	496-406 BC	AD 1000	1400 yrs	193
Homer (Iliad)	900 BC	400 BC	500 yrs	643
New Testament	AD 50 - AD 100	ca. AD 150	less than 100 years	5600

Modified from *Manuscript Evidence for Superior New Testament Reliability,* CHRISTIAN APOLOGETICS AND RESEARCH MINISTRY www.carm.org

The Critical Text Approach

Westcott & Hort

In 1881, B. F. Westcott and F. J. A. Hort published a critical text of the Greek New Testament using the uncial manuscripts as their primary source. This text omitted words or phrases that had been in the *Textus Receptus,* and listed them in the back as rejected

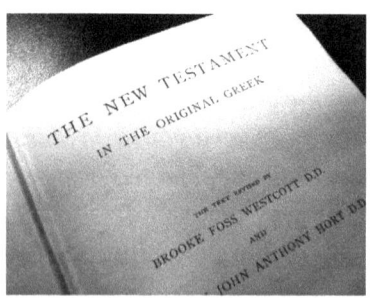

readings. There was no critical apparatus (i.e. a key indicating the evidence for variant readings). Around this same time an

How We Got the Bible

English Revision of the *King James* Bible, leaning heavily on this approach, was issued, known as the *Revised Version.* This text is used in the column of B. W. Johnson's *People's New Testament with Notes.* This was followed by an American version in 1901, the *American Standard Version.* Wescott and Hort held the theory that the *Textus Receptus* was an edited and expanded text changed by church fathers. This has remained an accepted view among many scholars to this day.

Modern Critical Texts

Since Westcott and Hort, the two most popular critical texts that follow the same approach are Nestle-Aland and the United Bible Society texts (sometimes classed together with the abbreviation NU). Both include a critical apparatus (that allows the reader to see the manuscript evidence for variants) and include new manuscript discoveries.

The "Majority Text" and the Byzantine Textform

In 1982, Zane Hodges and Arthur Farstad introduced a new approach to textual criticism that considered the weight of evidence for various readings rather than the age alone. The readings of their "Majority Text" are very similar to the *Textus Receptus* except in a very few passages. A similar approach was used in a text published in 2005 by Maurice A. Robinson and William G. Pierpont entitled *The New Testament in the Original Greek: Byzantine Textform.* Robinson and Pierpont found the "eclectic" texts produced by most critical editions troubling in the

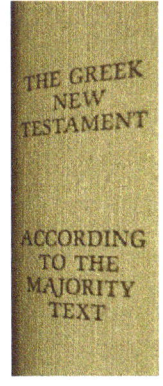

How We Got the Bible

fact that they form composite texts that are not representative of any actual manuscripts that have survived. Their approach focuses on the so-called "Byzantine Text-type" represented in the majority of Greek manuscripts that have survived.

"Test All Things"

It is appropriate to test the accuracy of manuscripts. Paul admonished Christians to, *"Test all things; hold fast what is good"* (1 Thess. 5:21). It is clear that there is an ever-present danger of apostasy. Paul warned, *"For the time will come when they will not endure sound doctrine, but according to their own desires because they have itching ears they will heap up for themselves teachers and they will turn their ears away from the truth and be turned aside to fables"* (1 Tim. 4:3, 4). As a result, it is right to make certain that copies of texts are accurate. It is right to make certain that translations are accurate. This does not reflect a lack of trust in God or the inspiration of Scripture.

Modern Translations

The Nature of Variants

Medieval Scribe

In discussing these textual variants we should clarify exactly what we are talking about. In the vast majority of instances the variants that we find will fall into one of three categories:

1. Spelling differences account for about 98% of the variants you find in New Testament manuscripts. An example of this is seen in Second Peter 1:2, which reads, "Grace and peace be multiplied to you in the knowledge of God and of Jesus our Lord." The Greek word translated "knowledge" here is *epignosis*

How We Got the Bible

(ἐπίγνωσις). Some manuscripts will spell the "i" sound differently. The standard spelling is simply with the Greek letter *iota* (the equivalent of the English letter *i*) whereas some will spell it with two letters, *epsilon* and *iota* (the equivalent of *ei*). This does not change the meaning, but simply reflects a different way to spell the same word. Another type of variant is when...

2. A word or phrase is omitted or substituted. This also is a rather common type of variant. You may find the word "Jesus" instead of the word "Christ." This type of variant may reflect the practice in some scriptoriums of copying a text as it was being read. While this could allow several copies to be produced at a time, it allowed for the possibility that a scribe could (innocently enough) substitute words that were synonyms. An example of this can be seen in Matthew 15:6. The *Textus Receptus* reads:

> ...Thus you have made the **commandment** of God of no effect by your tradition (Matt. 15:6, NKJV, emphasis mine).

While some manuscripts read:

> "...Thus you invalidated the **word** of God for the sake of your tradition (Matt. 15:6, NASB, emphasis mine).

Here most texts say "commandment," but some substitute "word." The meaning is essentially the same, but a variant exists nonetheless. The final type of variant which is more problematic and significant is when there is actually...

3. A Section omitted. Such is the case in the example we cited earlier of Mark chapter sixteen. When this occurs, the translator must evaluate the evidence that exists which supports the reading and what evidence discredits the reading. The choices that translators make regarding these kinds of variants will have a major effect on the difference in translations.

How We Got the Bible

The Effect on Translation

The question that the modern translator must ask (in essence) is this, "What effect Codex Sinaiticus (or other modern discoveries) should have on the textual basis used in a translation?" The translator must choose whether or not he will include standard readings in the body of the text or put variants in footnotes. The translator must decide which approach to textual criticism to take. Since the time of Westcott and Hort, editors of translations have been forced to choose between accepting the "critical text" approach or the *Textus Receptus*. In making such a choice, the translators must ask the question, "*Should age determine accuracy?*" If so, the translator will rely more on modern discoveries and modern critical editions. They must ask, "*Should the number and distribution of witnesses determine accuracy?*" If so, the translator will utilize either the *Textus Receptus* or the "Majority Text" approach. Of modern translations, the vast majority have accepted the "Critical Text" approach, as seen from the chart below.

Textual Basis of Modern Translations

Critical Text	Textus Receptus
* Revised Version (British) 1881 * American Standard 1901 * Revised Standard 1946 * New American Standard 1960 * New International Version 1978 * English Standard Version 2001	* New King James Version 1979

How We Got the Bible

Twentieth Century Discoveries

There are three major twentieth century discoveries we will consider to end our study:

- *Biblical Parchments and Papyri*
- *The Dead Sea Scrolls*
- *The Silver Scroll Pendant*

Biblical Parchments and Papyri

The Nash Papyrus. Four papyrus fragments of the Hebrew Old Testament were acquired by W. L. Nash and published in 1903. These dated to the second century BC, and contain portions of the ten commandments.

Nash Papyrus

Codex Washingtonensis (W). Was purchased from an Arab dealer near Cairo in 1906 and given to the Freer Gallery in Washington, DC. This parchment contains all the Gospels and dates from AD 350-400.

Codex Washingtonensis

The Nag Hammadi Library is a collection of fifty Gnostic papyri, with thirteen complete codices from the 300s. It was discovered in Egypt in 1945. Many of these Gnostic texts provide early witness to the New Testament texts from which they were altered.

The Nag Hammadi Library

How We Got the Bible

The Rylands Papyrus (P⁵²) is a fragment acquired by B.P. Grenfell in Egypt in 1920 and published in 1934. It belongs to the Rylands Library. It is dated to AD 150 and is the oldest undisputed fragment of a New Testament book containing a portion of John 18:31-33.

Rylands Papyrus

Chester Beatty Papyrus

The Chester Beatty Papyrus (P⁴⁶) was discovered in Egypt and sold to Chester Beatty and the University of Michigan in 1930s. This papyri contains almost all of Paul's epistles. When first discovered it was dated to around AD 200. Some modern scholars place it into the first century based upon paleography[3]

Other Papyri Discoveries

The twentieth century produced many other papyri discoveries of New Testament Greek manuscripts. Some of these predated Codex Sinaiticus and in some cases had readings closer to the *Textus Receptus.* This discredited the theory that *Textus Receptus* had been edited or expanded by church fathers.

New Testament Time Gaps

There never really was a 1400 year time gap in New Testament studies. Early New Testament manuscripts were known in the time of Erasmus and Stephanus. Yet, with the discovery of Sinaiticus

---

[3] See my article, "New Testament Manuscripts from the First Century," *Biblical Insights,* 2.9 (September 2002):13, 22, for more information.

How We Got the Bible

and the classification of other manuscripts, the gap was narrowed to fifty years. If P^{46} is in fact a first century manuscript there may be no gap! How true are the words of the Hebrew writer, *"Jesus Christ is the same yesterday, today, and forever"* (Heb. 13:8). How important it is for man to recognize that it is His word that will judge us on the Last Day. Jesus said, *"He who rejects Me, and does not receive My words, has that which judges him – the word that I have spoken will judge him in the last day"* (John 12:48).

The Dead Sea Scrolls

Old Testament Time gaps. The Aleppo Codex left a 1300 year time gap from the time the last book of the Old Testament was written until the earliest copy of an Old Testament manuscript. In the mid-twentieth century the most remarkable find of the century was uncovered which changed that significantly. In 1948, Sir Fredric Kenyon wrote:

> There is indeed, no probability that we shall ever find manuscripts of the Hebrew text going back to a period before the formation of the text which we know as Masoretic. We can only arrive at an idea of it by a study of the earliest translations made from it …(*Our Bible and the Ancient Manuscripts*, 1948 Printing).

Little did he know that discoveries would soon change this dramatically.

The Dead Sea Scrolls. In 1946 a Bedouin named Muhammad ed-Dib threw a stone into a cave looking for a goat that had wondered off. When he did so, he heard the sound of something breaking. Inside the cave was found pottery jars filled with manuscripts. Over the next decades, numerous caves with many other manuscripts were also discovered.

How We Got the Bible

These manuscripts were found to be a library of numerous religious and secular books stored away before the advance of the Roman armies upon Jerusalem in AD 70. These manuscripts date from 100 BC - AD 70. Among the scrolls were included biblical manuscripts of almost the entire the Hebrew Bible. When studied it was found that the text matched the Masoretic Text almost exactly. This changed the time gap from 1300 years to 300 years.

Dead Sea Scroll of the Psalms

The Psalmist declared, *"I will worship toward Your holy temple, and praise Your name for Your lovingkindness and Your truth; for you have magnified Your word above all your name"* (Ps. 138:2). There was another discovery that was to be made – that wasn't quite as dramatic, but perhaps even more remarkable.

The Silver Scroll Pendant

In 1979, in a tomb near the Old City in Jerusalem, a tomb was excavated and a small silver scroll necklace ornament was found with eighteen lines of Hebrew text dating from 600 BC. The scroll reads, from Numbers 6:24-26: *"The LORD bless you and keep you, the LORD make His face to shine upon you*

Silver Scroll Pendant

How We Got the Bible

and give you peace." This is the oldest biblical passage ever found. This changes the time gap once again. Now the gap is no longer 300 years—this scroll pendant was made before the Old Testament was completed. As a result, there is now no time gap!

We quoted earlier the words of Sir Fredric Kenyon who didn't foresee the Dead Sea Scroll discovery. As we end our study I want to quote him once again. He wrote:

> It is reassuring at the end to find that the general result of all these discoveries (of manuscripts) and all this study is to strengthen the proof of the authenticity of the Scriptures and our conviction that we have in our hands the veritable Word of God (From *The Story of the Bible,* quoted in Josh McDowell's *Evidence that Demands a Verdict).*

The Psalmist declared, *"Your word is a lamp unto my feet and a light to my path"* (Ps. 119:105). How true these words remain to this very day. The word of God, the gospel of Jesus Christ remains the way to salvation. We close our study with Paul's words, *"For I am not ashamed of the gospel of Christ, for it is the power of God unto salvation for everyone who believes, for the Jew first and also for the Greek"* (Rom. 1:16).

Discussion Questions

1. What is meant by the *Textual Basis* of a translation?
2. To what does the phrase *Textus Receptus* refer?
3. What is *Codex Sinaiticus* and when and where was it discovered?
4. What are some factors that can give us great confidence in the reliability of biblical texts?
5. What are the *Dead Sea Scrolls* and when and where were they discovered?

Appendix: Choosing a Translation

We have considered the process which led to the formation and preservation of Scripture. *Where do we go from here?* Unless we have had the opportunity to study Greek or Hebrew, we are forced to rely upon English translations. How do we choose a good translation for the study of God's word? First, let's review what makes one translation different from another.

Why Do Translations Differ?

We noted earlier some reasons why translations differ.

1. *Differences in language.* Languages communicate different things in different ways. Idiomatic expressions can be unique to a particular language. How can these ideas be carried into another language? Even within the same language, meaning can change over time.

2. *A different textual basis.* If a translation relies on modern discoveries, variants will occur. A word will be added or left off. One translation may say "Christ" where another says "Jesus." These variants should not lead one to doubt the reliability of the text. Most biblical variants involve minor differences in word order, spelling, and synonymous wording.

3. *Different doctrinal perspectives.* No matter how one might try to avoid it, we can not remove ourselves from the influence our own beliefs have on our choices. If I am translating something and encounter a couple of ways something could be rendered—one which supports my beliefs and another which does not, I am mostly likely to choose the alternative that supports my beliefs.

4. *Style of translation.* There are at least four styles of translation. We can illustrate with a brief survey of some English translations how different philosophies of translation affect the outcome, value, and profitability of a translation for use in Bible study.

How We Got the Bible

Different Styles of Translation

The Paraphrase. To paraphrase something, is literally to state something "beside" (Gr. *para*) something else. It is to summarize a text or put it in one's own words. All preaching involves paraphrase. A preacher must explain a text as he understands it—in his own words. The apostle Paul, paraphrased Isaiah 64:4-5 through Divine inspiration in 1 Corinthians 2:9. The ancient Jewish texts called the *Targums* were interpretations and paraphrases of Old Testament books. The Greek scholar Desiderius Erasmus, whose work laid the foundation of the *King James Version*, did his own paraphrase of the New Testament.

Paraphrase is not translation in the strictest sense, in that it does not attempt to bring the exact words or thoughts of one language into another. Yet, it is a method employed in translation of biblical and secular texts. It is not sinful in and of itself. However, of all styles of translation it is the most vulnerable to bias, misinterpretation, and blatant error because it is *the words of man* about *the word of God,* and not *the word of God* itself. Modern times have seen two major examples of Biblical paraphrases:

***The Living Bible* (also known as *The Book,* or *The Way*), by Kenneth Taylor. Wheaton, IL: Tyndale House Pub., 1971.** Taylor was a Baptist who first began writing paraphrases to explain Scripture to his children. This eventually led to a complete paraphrase of the entire Bible. Taylor was conservative, but many of his paraphrases reflected his Calvinistic background. For example, he rendered Psalm 51:5, *"But I was born a sinner, yes, from the moment my mother conceived me."* The Hebrew says, *"I was brought forth in sin"* but it does not specify if his own, his mother's, or the world's sin is meant. The Bible does not teach inherited sin (Ezek. 18:20). This same bias is seen in Romans 5:12, that reads, *"When Adam sinned, sin entered the entire human race. His sin spread death throughout all the world, so everything began to grow old and die, for all sinned."* The Greek says, *"through one man sin entered the world,"* going on to explain that "death" (not physical, but spiritual death) *"spread to all, because all sinned."* Here Paul uses the same form of the word for sin that is found in Romans 3:23, *"for all have sinned and fall short of the glory of God."* It is a different thing to say sin entered *the world,* than to say it *"entered the human race."*

How We Got the Bible

The Message, by Eugene Peterson. Colorado Springs: NavPress Pub. Group, 1993. Peterson, a former Presbyterian preacher, and professor at Regents College in British Columbia, did his own paraphrase with no verse divisions as an evangelistic tool. It is much less conservative than the *Living Bible,* employing modern idioms totally foreign to the original text. In Matthew 9:23, Peterson changes the *"fluteplayers"* and *"noisy crowd wailing"* to *"neighbors bringing in casseroles."* In Acts 2:41 he says of the 3000 who were baptized and *"added to"* them that *"they were baptized and were signed up."* Where does Scripture teach a *signing-up* to obey the gospel?

We might see these examples as innocent enough, but a paraphrase can fuel error. For example, In Matthew 16:18 Peterson has Jesus telling Peter, *"You are Peter, a rock. This is the rock on which I will put together my church."* This is exactly what Roman Catholics claim with regard to Peter, in defense of their claim that Peter was the first "pope." What this paraphrase fails to bring out is that Jesus uses two different words here for "rock," inferring that it is the confession Peter made, not Peter himself, upon which the church is built. Peterson also reveals his Calvinistic leanings, rendering Ephesians 2:8, *"Saving is all his idea, and all his work. All we do is trust him enough to let him do it."* The uninformed may come to believe from such words that salvation is by faith alone, or that even faith is something God forces upon man. This is not what the Bible teaches (cf. James 2:24). From these examples we must conclude, while one might consult a paraphrase to consider human opinion on Scripture it should never be used as our primary scriptural source.

Interlinear Translation. If we thought of paraphrase as one extreme on a scale, the other extreme would be what is called an "interlinear" translation. An interlinear places an English word-for-word translation under every word in the original language. Whenever possible, one word is under the word in the original language. The challenges to this approach are: 1) Not all foreign words can be translated by a single word. 2) Word order is dramatically different from one language to another. Finally, 3) Some original language words are grammatical markers and have no corresponding equivalent in English. Because of these challenges, interlinear translations are good study tools, but far too awkward for use in teaching, reading, or preaching. One of the most readily available interlinear Bibles is *The Interlinear Bible,* by Jay P. Green. Grand Rapids: Baker Book House, 1982. Green utilizes the *Textus Receptus* as his textual basis for the New Testament. Modern printings of this translation even include Strong's numbering below each original language word.

How We Got the Bible

"Dynamic Equivalence" (*thought for thought*). A step away from a paraphrase is an approach known as *dynamic equivalence* or "thought for thought" translation. This approach is more dependent than a paraphrase upon the actual text of the original language, but it allows itself more flexibility to express the meaning (or what the translators believe to be the meaning) of the text. All translation involves some degree of this. For example, most translations of 2 John 12 read, *"I hope to come to you and speak face to face."* This is a good dynamic equivalence translation, but the Greek literally says "mouth to mouth." Obviously, that means something different in English than it did in Koine Greek. The judgments translators make about how much freedom to allow themselves in this determines whether a translation moves closer or further away from a paraphrase. The problem is the more freedom that editors allow themselves, the more vulnerable the text becomes to bias, misinterpretation, and error. We can illustrate this with the more extreme examples of dynamic equivalence translations and move towards a more literal approach.

The Voice New Testament. **Nashville: Thomas Nelson Pub., 2008.** One problem with many dynamic equivalence translations is their reliance upon gimmicks to attract an audience. This relatively new project, called *The Voice,* presents the text of the New Testament in screenplay format. It uses the term *"Liberating King"* throughout in place of *"Christ."* Instead of *"baptism"* it refers to *"ceremonial washing"* with a footnote in each place that it literally means *"to immerse."* Baptism is immersion, but it doesn't clarify misunderstandings about baptism by calling it a *"ceremonial washing."*

Although *The Voice* does not present itself as a paraphrase, it incorporates so much commentary into the text that it becomes a paraphrase. For example, many translations use the custom of italicizing words supplied by editors. Notice how *The Voice* renders Acts 20:7:

> The Sunday night before our Monday departure, we gathered to celebrate the breaking of bread. *Many wondrous events happened as Paul traveled, ministering among the churches. One evening a most unusual event occurred.*

Two complete sentences are added by the editors. This is commentary, not translation!

How We Got the Bible

The Amplified Bible, **ed. Francis E. Siewert and twelve other scholars. Lockman Foundation. Grand Rapids: Zondervan Pub., 1965.** This text attempted to bring out some of the nuances that can be found in certain grammatical forms in the original language. In some places this has merit. For example, in Matthew 18:18, it reads, *"Truly I tell you, whatever you forbid and declare to be improper and unlawful on earth must be what is already forbidden in heaven, and whatever you permit and declare proper and lawful on earth must be what is already permitted in heaven."* This is a valuable analysis. In this text the Greek future with the perfect literally expresses *"will be in a state of having been bound."*

In other cases, however, this approach allows itself too much room for commentary. For example, in Psalm 51:5 it reads, *"Behold, I was brought forth in [a state of] iniquity; my mother was sinful who conceived me [and I too am sinful]."* In 1 Peter 3:21 it goes so far as to render this passage, *"And baptism, which is a figure [of their deliverance], does now also save you [from inward questionings and fears], not by the removing of outward body filth [bathing], but by [providing you with] the answer of a good and clear conscience (inward cleanness and peace) before God [because you are demonstrating what you believe to be yours] through the resurrection of Jesus Christ."* This presents denominational commentary as if it is expressed in the grammar of the text. It is not!

The American (and United) Bible Society, the major publishers of foreign language translations, have done two dynamic equivalence translations:

The Good News Bible **(aka.** *Today's English Version***), Robert Bratcher (NT) and six others (OT). New York: American Bible Society, 1976.** This translation was written on a six grade reading level and made broad use of interpretation rather than actual translation. We see this in a text we considered above—Acts 20:7 reads, *"On Saturday evening we gathered together for the fellowship meal."* The Greek text says, *"first of the sabbaths,"* using the plural of the word *sabbath* to refer to a week. The idea is thus, the *"first day of the week."* It is true that by some Jewish reckoning a day started on the night before, but the text does not explicitly identify this accounting of time. Further, in calling this *"the fellowship meal"* it reads into the text the false view that Christians first combined a full meal with the Lord's Supper. First Corinthians 11:17-34 condemns this.

The Contemporary English Version. **New York: American Bible Society, 1995.** This text used more translators than *The Good News Bible,* but it was still

How We Got the Bible

aimed at a children's reading level. This text yielded to the mounting pressure exerted by feminists to eliminate "gender specific" references in Scripture. In Ephesians 5:22 the command to wives to *"submit"* was changed to a charge to, *"put their husbands first."* 1 Corinthians 11:10, in Paul's discussion of the head covering, reference to a *"sign of authority"* is changed to *"a sign of her authority."* Finally, in 1 Timothy 3:3 and 3:12 qualifications for elders and deacons in the church restricted to those who are *"the husband of one wife"* is opened to those *"faithful in marriage."* That is not what the text says. These are alterations of the inspired text.

New Living Translation. **Wheaton, IL: Tyndale House Pub., 1996 (rev. 2004).** In 1996 Tyndale House, under the guidance of Mark Taylor (one of Kenneth Taylor's sons) published a new work entitled the *New Living Translation*. This project sought to retain the readability of the older *Living Bible* while avoiding the stigma of being a paraphrase. Their initial efforts met with some success, but in 2004 Tyndale House issued a revision of the *New Living Translation* which (in some cases) became more of a paraphrase than the original *Living Bible.* Both the original *Living Bible* and the 1996 edition of the *New Living Translation* were fairly literal in their rendering of Acts 2:38. Both described baptism as *"for the remission of sins."* The 2004 edition, however, went beyond the point of paraphrase and read its own biased commentary into the text. It has Peter commanding the people to, *"be baptized in the name of Jesus Christ to show that you have received forgiveness of sins."* This is outrageous!

Holman Christian Standard Bible. **Nashville: Holman Bible Publishers, 2004.** Given the dangers of bias and misinterpretation in dynamic equivalence translation, some have sought to attain a balance between a "word-for-word" and a "thought-for-thought" approach. Under the influence of the Southern Baptist convention, Holman Publishers produced what it calls an "optimal equivalence" translation. In theory this effort is commendable, however, in practice, there is still denominational bias that reveals itself. Once again, in Psalm 51:5 it reads, *"Indeed, I was guilty [when I] was born; I was sinful when my mother conceived me."* Scripture does not teach that anyone is born "guilty." Only a few Psalms before in this the same translation David said, *"I was given over to You at birth; You have been my God from my mother's womb"* (Psalm 22:10). How can David be "guilty" and yet "given over" to God at the same time? It renders Acts 22:16: *"And now, why delay? Get up and be baptized, and wash away your sins by calling on His name."* Calling on the name of the Lord is more than just saying words. It is a complete commitment (cf. Rom. 10:13). Even so, many denominations teach that it is prayer, and that one can

How We Got the Bible

be saved "by calling on his name *in prayer*" (*The Voice*). To read this into this text denies the role baptism plays in forgiveness and reflects denominational teaching and not Scripture.

The New International Version. **International Bible Society. Grand Rapids: Zondervan Pub., 1978.** This has become the most popular translation among Protestants in America. It did not absolutely reject the *Textus Receptus,* but relied heavily on critical editions of the Greek New Testament. While it promotes itself as the product of translators from various religious views, it demonstrates a blatant Calvinistic bias. This is seen clearly in Romans 8:5, which reads, *"Those who live according to the sinful nature have their minds set on what that nature desires..."* The Greek word *sarx* means simply "flesh." Jesus shared the same *sarx* with mankind, yet He had no "sinful nature" (cf. Heb. 2:14). It is a reflection of the Calvinistic doctrine of Total Hereditary Depravity to speak of this as the "sinful nature." Thankfully, the most recent edition of the NIV has corrected this to read simply "flesh."

The *New International Version,* in the last few decades has become embroiled in controversy over gender-neutral language. In 1996 the International Bible Society issued an "inclusive language edition" with gender-neutral language. This roused fierce opposition among religious leaders in America, forcing them to alter publication in the United States. This did not stop their efforts to yield to this growing feminist pressure. The original *New International Version* rendered Psalm 8:4, *"What is man that you are mindful of him, the son of man that you care for him?"* However, an edition they released in 1994 called the *New International Reader's Edition*, aimed at children reads, *"What is a human being that you think about him? What is a son of man that you take care of him?"* In this version only the first phrase was changed to read *"human beings"* for *"man.* "Their most recent release in 2005, called *Today's New International Version* abandons all gender references, reading, *"What are mere mortals that you are mindful of them, human beings that you care for them?"* This might seem innocent enough in this text, but it reflects a willingness to reject gender distinctions, roles, and references that are present in the original text in response to modern prejudices and preferences. We don't have that right!

The Dangers of Dynamic Equivalent Translation. Leland Ryken, in his work entitled, *Choosing a Bible,* offers "Five Negative Effects of Dynamic Equivalence." These are: 1) *Taking Liberties in Translation;* 2) *Destabilization of the Text;* 3) *What the Bible "Means" vs. What the Bible Says;* 4) *Falling*

How We Got the Bible

Short of What We Should Expect; and 5) *A Logical and Linguistic Impossibility.* He offers the following observations in this section:

> Dynamic equivalent translators believe that the translator has the duty to make interpretive decisions for the ignorant reader. Eugene Nida, for example, claims that "the average reader is usually much less capable of making correct judgments about . . . alternative meanings than is the translator, who can make use of the best scholarly judgments on ambiguous passages." But if this is true, why is it that translators, with their allegedly superior and reliable knowledge, cannot agree among themselves? Instead of leading the Bible reading public into a better grasp of the original text, dynamic equivalent translations have confused the public by multiplying the range of renditions of various Bible passages (15).

Commenting on the fact that dynamic equivalence translations remove indications of the actual wording of a text, Ryken quotes, Ray Van Leeuwen, from his article "We Really Do Need Another Translation," writing:

> It is hard to know what the Bible *means* when we are uncertain about what it *says*. . . . The problem with [functional equivalent] translations (i.e., most modern translations) is that they prevent the reader from inferring biblical *meaning* because they change what the Bible *said* (17).

We agree wholeheartedly! Because of the danger of bias, misinterpretation, and error, a dynamic equivalence (or thought for thought) translation should not be used in teaching, preaching, public reading, or as a primary source in Bible study.

"Formal Equivalence" (*word for word*). A "formal equivalent" (or literal) translation seeks to overcome the awkwardness of an interlinear translation while representing the actual content of the original text. Whenever possible, a word for word equivalence is established in language that is clear, but parallel to the content of the original. The degree to which a text maintains this correspondence moves it up or down on the scale between dynamic equivalence and an interlinear.

No translation is flawless, however, translations that seek to establish a formal equivalence between the original language and the English translation

How We Got the Bible

are less prone to bias, misinterpretation, and blatant error. In our consideration earlier in this text, we followed the steps that led to the publication of the *King James Version*. While recent years have seen renewed interest in pre-King James translations, we will start our consideration of literal or formal equivalence translations with a consideration of the *King James Version*.

King James Version (or *Authorized Version*). This translation was produced in 1611 by 47 scholars under the authority of King James I. In 1873, it was revised by the Church of England into the form generally used today. Undoubtedly, the *King James Version* is the most influential English Bible in history. Based on the *Textus Receptus* in the New Testament, it built upon the earlier works of Tyndale and others, while avoiding sectarian commentary and over-reliance on the Vulgate. It remains the basis for countless Bible study resources and has shaped the vocabulary of religious discourse in English.

While the *King James Version* is a wonderful literal translation that preserves the content and basic structure of the original languages, it does have some weaknesses. First, it consistently translates the Greek *hades* and Hebrew *sheol* as "hell." In Acts 2:31, it speaks of, *"...the resurrection of Christ, that his soul was not left in hell..."* Both *hades* and *sheol* do not refer to final judgment, but to the place of the dead prior to judgment (cf. Rev. 20:13-14). Second, it uses names and expressions that are anachronistic (i.e. misplaced in terms of time). In Acts 12:4 it describes plans concerning Paul, that they were *"...intending after Easter to bring him forth to the people."* The Greek word *pascha* refers to the Jewish feast of Passover, and not to *"Easter,"* which was a man-made development after the New Testament as a memorial of Christ's death.

The *King James Version* also included a doubtful passage in the body of the text. 1 John 5:7 (the so-called *Johannnine Comma*) reads, *"For there are three that bear record in heaven, the Father, the Word, and the Holy Ghost: and these three are one."* While this text reflects a truth taught in the New Testament, it is not found in any Greek manuscripts prior to the eleventh century nor in the most ancient translations. It was not in Erasmus' first editions of the Greek New Testament and was only added when a late Greek manuscript (which had it added from Latin) was brought to him.[1]

---

[1] For more on this, see my article, "The Johannnine Comma," *Focus Magazine Online* (April 28, 2016) [online] https://focusmagazine.org/the-johannine-comma.php.

How We Got the Bible

Finally, the *King James Version* uses language that has changed meaning over the 400 years since it was first produced. Lewis Foster, in his book *Selecting a Translation of the Bible,* points out the following examples:

Obsolete words:
Carriages (Acts 21:15) means *baggage.*
Script (Mark 6:8) means *wallet* or *bag.*
Fetched a compass (Acts 28:13) means *sailed around.*

Changes of meaning:
Letteth (2 Thess. 2:7) means *restrains.*
Prevent (1 Thess. 4:15) means *precede.*
Charger (Mark 6:25) means *platter.*
Conversation (James 3:13) means *conduct.*

I have a book in my library called *The Language of the King James Bible,* that is essentially a dictionary defining the meaning of the Middle English wording used in the *King James Version* to assist modern English readers. This is a serious obstacle when it comes to teaching, preaching, and private study. To resolve this, a number of modernized versions of the *King James Version* have been produced. The most popular of these is…

The New King James Version. **Nashville: Thomas Nelson Pub. , 1982.** This translation retains the style and flow of the *King James Version* while eliminating obsolete words and expressions. It is close enough to the original *King James Version* that the reader can readily use resources based on the *King James* without confusion. The *New King James Version* is not perfect. It retains the doubtful text of 1 John 5:7. Some see its use of *Textus Receptus* as a "weakness." In my judgment, it is a rash conclusion to assume that any manuscript that is older is necessarily closer to the original. Such a conclusion presumes that flawed or altered manuscripts would receive the same wear and usage that accurate manuscripts would receive. That is a dangerous assumption. Even so, the *New King James Version* cites in footnotes all pertinent evidence from modern discoveries.

I believe that the *New King James Version* is the best choice currently available that maintains a connection to the vocabulary, influence, and resources of the *King James Version* while using contemporary English that corresponds directly to the wording and structure of the original text. It is literal without being awkward. It is readable while demonstrating the content of the original text.

American Standard Version **1901.** This was the first American translation that used nineteenth century manuscript discoveries in a revision of the *King James*

How We Got the Bible

Version. It was one of the most literal translations ever done, even to the point that it was somewhat awkward to read. It broke the convention of translating the Hebrew name for God as "L{\sc ord}" and rendered it instead "Jehovah." It retained the Old English forms "thee" and "ye" to distinguish singular and plural forms of the second person pronoun. The *American Standard Version* was widely used by many in the twentieth century. Now it has become harder and harder to find in print. Only Star Bible Publications, Euless, Texas currently publishes this edition. Electronic versions are available in many Bible programs and through online Bible websites.

New American Standard Bible. **Lockman Foundation. 1971, rev. 1995.** To overcome the awkwardness of the *American Standard Version* and to utilize discoveries made since its publication, the *New American Standard Bible* was produced by the Lockman Foundation. It remained highly literal but improved the readability of the *American Standard Version*, utilizing more contemporary vocabulary. The *New American Standard Bible* is an excellent translation, but it moves some readings of the *Textus Receptus* into the footnotes. This, becomes awkward in study when such readings are encountered.

Revised Standard. **Nashville: Thomas Nelson Pub., 1952.** This text was the first revision of the *Tyndale-King James-American Standard* tradition produced by liberal scholars for the National Council of Churches. Its translators did not hold a conservative view of inspiration. H. Leo Boles, the Gospel preacher who authored the commentary of Matthew for the Gospel Advocate Commentary series, was asked to participate in its production and declined after one meeting. This liberalism demonstrated itself in passages such as Isaiah 7:14. Instead of affirming the prophecy of the virgin birth (quoted in Matthew 1:23) it rendered the passage, *"Therefore the Lord himself will give you a sign. Behold, a young woman shall conceive and bear a son, and shall call his name Imman'u-el."*

New Revised Standard Version. **The Division of Christian Education of the National Council of Churches, 1989.** In 1989 the National Council of Churches produced a revision of the *Revised Standard Version* that utilized discoveries made since the original edition. It retained the liberal elements of the *Revised Standard Version* such as *"young woman"* in Isaiah 7:14 and moved closer to dynamic equivalence by incorporating gender-neutral language in references to humans while retaining masculine references in to Deity.

English Standard Version. **Standard Bible Society. Wheaton, IL: Crossway Books and Bibles, 2001.** This is one of the newest formal equivalence translations that describes itself as "essentially literal" striving to be "transparent

How We Got the Bible

to the original text." The *English Standard Version* is very similar to the *New American Standard Bible*. It utilizes the same textual basis and maintains a conservative "word for word" correspondence to the original text. It has deliberately resisted efforts to impose gender-neutral language into the text. Unfortunately, the editors of the *English Standard Version* made the decision not to follow the custom of italicizing wording supplied by translators. This can lead the reader to think that a word or phrase (that may be inferred in the text) is actually present when it is not. An example of this may be seen Romans 8:5. Its translation reads, *"For those who live according to the flesh set their minds on the things of the flesh, but those who live according to the Spirit set their minds on the things of the Spirit."* This is an accurate translation, but it duplicates the words *"set their minds on"* when the Greek does not. If this was in italics it would be clear and would truly make it "transparent to the original text." The *English Standard Version* is also inconsistent in some choices. In Matthew 16:18 it incorrectly translates *hades, "hell"* even though it renders it *"hades"* in Acts 2:31 and Luke 16:23. In spite of these shortcomings, the *English Standard Version* maintains a careful respect for the original text and avoids biased translation of controversial passages.

Recommended Translations. Translation is a difficult matter. While the student of the Scripture should use great caution regarding the choice of a translation, we should never imagine that God's word cannot be understood in its simplicity. Even the worst translation generally preserves the force of this simplicity. Even so, because of the danger that paraphrase and dynamic equivalence translations risk in bringing bias, misinterpretation, and error into the text, such versions should never be used as our primary source in study, teaching, preaching, or reading. Among formal equivalence translations, the *Revised Standard,* and *New Revised Standard* demonstrate a far too liberal view of inspiration and gender distinctions. Although the *English Standard Version* would have been stronger with the use of italics to indicate editorial editions, it stands with the *King James Version, American Standard, New American Standard,* and *New King James Version* as excellent translations for study, reading, preaching, and teaching. In my judgment, by retaining readings from the *Textus Receptus,* while noting variants in the footnotes, the *New King James Version* is the most useful formal equivalence translation.

Index

1QIsa[a] 12
"42 Line" Bible 49
Aaron ben Asher 64, 65
Aldhelm 52
Alexander the Great 19
Alexandrinus, Codex (A) 68, 71
Alfred, King 52
Aleppo Codex 64, 65, 79
Alphabet 7, 8
American Standard Version (1901) . . .
. . . . 73, 76, 91, 92, 93
Amplified Bible 86
Apocrypha 20, 21, 39
Apostolic Fathers 33, 35, 39
Aramaic 5, 23, 24
Aristeas, Letter of 19
Armenian 44
Athanasius, Letter of 40
Babylonian Talmud 13, 21
Bede 52
Beza, Theodore 68
Bezae, Codex (D) 68
Bishops' Bible (1568) 58, 60
Calvin, John 57, 58, 68
Cambridge 50, 54, 59, 68
Canon 16, 17, 18, 30, 31
Canon Lists 37, 38
Charles I, King of England 68
Chester Beatty Papyrus (P[46]) . . . 78, 79
"Christian" Humanism 49, 67
Clement of Rome 32, 33
Clementine Vulgate 57
Codex 6, 25
Constantine, Emperor 39
Contemporary English Bible (1995). 86, 87

Coptic 43
Coverdale Bible (1535) 55
Coverdale, Miles 55, 57
Cranmer, Thomas 56, 57
Critical Apparatus 73
Critical Texts 72, 73, 76
Cromwell, Thomas 55, 56
Cuneiform 7
Cyril 44, 45
Cyrillic 44, 45
Damasus, Bishop of Rome 46
Dana and Mantey 24
Dead Sea Scrolls . . 12, 21, 62, 77, 79, 80
Documentary Hypothesis 10, 11
Dynamic Inspiration 4
Dynamic Equivalence . 62, 85, 86, 87, 88
Ecclesiasticus 17
Edward VI, King of England 53
en-Dib, Muhammad 79
English Standard Version (2001) . . . . .
. . . . 76, 92, 93
Elizabeth I, Queen of England . . 53, 58
Elziver 66
Ephraemi Rescriptus, Codex (C) . . . 69
Epistle of Barnabas 33, 39
Erasmus, Desiderius 50, 54, 65, 83
Estienne, Robert (Stephanus) . . . 50, 66
Ethiopic 44
Eusebius 29, 33, 34
Ezra, The Prophet. 9, 10, 14, 15, 20, 45
"Formal Equivalence" Translation . . . .
. . . . 89, 90, 91, 92, 93
Geneva Bible 57, 58, 60
"Gender-Neutral" Language . 88, 92, 93
Ge'ez 44

How We Got the Bible

Gnosticism 33, 34, 35, 36
Goodspeed, Edgar J. 29
Good News Bible (1976) 86
Gospels. 27, 28
Gospel of Judas 36, 37
Gospel of Mary Magdalene 36
Gospel of Thomas 35
Gothic 43, 44
Great Assembly (or Synagogue) 15, 16
Great Bible (1539) 55, 56, 59
Greek 5, 19, 23, 24, 25, 67, 74, 75
Grenfell, B.P. 78
Gutenberg, Johannes 49
Hebrew. 5, 23, 64
Henry VIII, King of England . . . .
. . . . 53, 55, 56
Hieroglyphic Script 7
Hodges, Zane and Arthur Farstad . . 73
Holman Christian Standard (2004) . . . .
. . . . 87, 88
Holy Spirit 3, 4, 25, 27, 28, 29
Ideographic Scripts 7
Ignatius of Antioch 32
Immanuel 25
Indulgences, Sale of 49, 51
Inspiration, Divine 3, 4, 27, 28
The Interlinear Bible 84
Interlinear Translation 84
Irenaeus, of Lyons 27, 28, 36
James I, King of England. 53, 59
Jamnia, Council of 18
Jerome 39, 45, 46
Jesus Christ 20, 26, 75
Johnson, B.W. 73
Josephus 11, 17, 20
Josiah, King of Judah   9, 11, 12, 13, 14
Justin Martyr 31, 32
Kenyon, Sir Fredric 79, 81
Koine Greek 5, 23, 24, 85
Ketubim 16, 17
King James Version (1611) . . . .
. . . . 59, 60, 73, 90, 91, 93
Laodicia, Synod of 40
Latin Vulgate 45, 46, 50, 57, 58

Leningrad Codex 65
Lindisfarne Gospels 52
Literal Translation 62, 89, 90, 91
Living Bible (1971) 83, 87
Lollards 52
Logia 29
Lucar, Cyril 68
Luther, Martin 47, 51, 55
LXX (Septuagint). . . . .
. . . . 12, 13, 19, 20, 21, 24
Maimonides 65
"Majority Text" 71, 73, 76
Majuscule. 25, 67
Manetho 11
Marcion 36, 37
Martin, Gregory 58
Mary I, Queen of England . . 53, 56, 57
Masorah 64
Masoretes 64, 65
Masoretic Text 63, 64, 65, 79
Matthew's Bible (1537) 55
Matthew, Thomas. 55
Mesrop 44
The Message (1993). 84
Messiah 25, 26, 61
Methodius 44
Metzger, Bruce 31
Minuscules 25, 67
Mishnah, Jewish. 15
Moses 7, 9, 10, 11, 15, 17
Nag Hammadi Library 77
Nash Papyrus 77
Nestle-Aland Greek NT 73
Neviim 16, 17
New American Standard Bible (1960) .
. . . . 61, 63, 75, 76, 92, 93
New King James Version (1979) . . . . .
. . . . 61, 63, 75, 76, 91, 93
New International Reader's Version (1994). 88
New International Version (1978) . 76. 88
New Living Translation (1996) 87
New Revised Standard Version (1989) .
. . . . 92, 93

How We Got the Bible

The New Testament in the Original Greek: Byzantine Textform (2005)..... 73
Nicea, Council of 39
Origen of Alexandria 29
P⁴⁶, Chester Beatty Papyrus ... 78, 79
Pache, René 4
Palimpsest 69
Papias of Hierapolis 29, 32
Papyrus............ 6, 25, 48, 77, 78
Paraphrase 62. 83
Parchment 6, 25
Parker, Matthew................ 58
People's New Testament with Notes .. 73
Peshitta 43
Philo of Alexandria 17
Pierpont, William G. 73
Plenary Inspiration............... 4
Pope Clement VIII.............. 57
Pope Martin V 53
Printing Press............... 48, 49
Proto-Siniatic Alphabet 8
Pseudepigrapha 21
Ptolemy II..................... 19
Puritans 57, 58, 59
Q Hypothesis 28, 29
Quelle....................... 28
Revised Version (1881) 72, 76
Revised Standard Version (1946).....
.... 76, 92, 93
Rheims-Douay Bible (1582) 58
Robinson, Maurice A. 73
Rogers, John................ 55, 57
Rylands Papyrus (P⁵²) 78
Scrivner 66
Scrolls 6, 12
Septuagint (LXX)..12, 13, 19, 20, 21, 24
Shepherd of Hermas.......... 33, 34

Shlomo ben Buya'a 65
Slavonic, "Old Church" 44, 45
Silver Scroll Pendant 77, 80, 81
Sinaiticus, Codex (א). 69, 70, 71, 75, 78
Sola Scriptura 51
Stephanus, Robert (Estienne)... 50, 66
Streeter, B. H. 28
Syriac 43
Tablets 5, 6
Targums 83
Tatian's Diatessaron.......... 34, 35
Tertullian 33, 34
Textual Basis 61, 62, 63, 76, 82
Textus Receptus 50, 62, 63, 65, 66, 70, 72, 73, 75, 76, 78, 82. 84, 88, 90, 91, 92, 93
Tischendorf, Constantin.... 69, 70, 71
Today's New International Version (2005) . 88
Torah 16, 17
Trent, Council of 57
Tyndale Bible (1526) 54, 55, 59
Tyndale, William 54, 55
Uncials.................... 25, 67
United Bible Society Greek NT.... 73
Valla, Lorenzo 50
Vaticanus, Codex (B) 68, 71
Verbal Inspiration................ 4
The Voice (2008) 85. 88
Vulgate, Latin...... 45, 46, 50, 57, 58
Washingtonensis, Codex (W)...... 77
Watts, Isaac 42
Wellhausen, Julius 10
Westcott, B. F. and F. J. A. Hort... 72, 76
Whittingham, William 57
Wulfilas 43, 44
Wycliffe, John 52, 53
Wycliffe, Bible........... 52, 53, 55

Scripture Index

Genesis 49:10 26
Exodus 20:3 .... 8, 9
Exodus 31:18 6
Leviticus 27:34. 9
Numbers 6:24-26 .... 80, 81
Deuteronomy 18:15 25
Deuteronomy 28:61 12
Deuteronomy 29:1 10
Deuteronomy 29:21 12
Deuteronomy 30:10 12
Deuteronomy 31:26 12
Joshua 1:8. 12
Joshua 8:31, 34 12
Joshua 22:11. 12
2 Kings 22:8 12
2 Kings 22:11 13
2 Kings 23:1-3 14
2 Chronicles 17:9. 12
2 Chronicles 34:14 12
Ezra 7:6 14
Ezra 7:10 14
Nehemiah 8:1 .... 10, 12
Nehemiah 8:1-8 15
Nehemian 8:3 12
Nehemiah 8:8 45
Nehemiah 9:3 12
Psalm 8:4 88
Psalm 22:10 87
Psalm 34:20 26
Psalm 51:5 .... 86, 87
Psalm 119:89 13
Psalm 119:105 81
Psalm 138:2 80
Isaiah 7:14 .... 25, 92
Isaiah 9:1-2. 26
Isaiah 9:7 26
Isaiah 40:8 13
Isaiah 53:9 26
Isaiah 55:11 65
Isaiah 64:4-5. 83
Jeremiah 17:1 .... 5, 6
Jeremiah 36:2 6
Ezekiel 2:9 6
Ezekiel 18:20 .... 58, 83
Daniel 2:44. 67
Daniel 9:25. 26
Hosea 4:6 48
Micah 5:2 26
Zechariah 12:10 26
Malachi 4:4 10
Matthew 5:18 .... 13, 38
Matthew 7:15 34
Matthew 9:23 84
Matthew 15:6 75
Matthew 16:15-17 26
Matthew 16:18 84
Matthew 18:18 86
Matthew 23:13 48
Matthew 24:35 .... 13, 68
Matthew 27:46 24
Matthew 28:19-20 27
Mark 5:41 24

How We Got the Bible

Mark 6:8. 91	1 Corinthians 2:13 28
Mark 6:25. 91	1 Corinthians 11:10 87
Mark 12:26. 10	1 Corinthians 11:17-34. 86
Mark 16:9-20 . . . . 70, 71, 75	1 Corinthians 14:37 27
Mark 16:15,16 45	Galatians 3:10 12
Luke 16:23 93	Ephesians 2:8 84
Luke 24:44 17	Ephesians 3:4 52
John 1:17 11	Ephesians 5:9 63
John 4:25-26. 26	Ephesians 5:22 87
John 7:19 . . . . 10, 11	1 Thessalonians 2:13 3
John 12:48 79	1 Thessalonians 4:15 91
John 14:26 . . . . 27, 28	1 Thessalonians 5:21 . . . . . . 46, 74
John 16:13 27	2 Thessalonians 2:7 91
John 18:31-33. 78	1 Timothy 3:3. 87
Acts 2:31 90	1 Timothy 3:12. 87
Acts 2:38 . . . . 59, 60, 87	1 Timothy 3:15. 54
Acts 2:41 84	1 Timothy 4:3, 4. . . . . . . 34, 46, 74
Acts 12:4 90	2 Timothy 3:15. 52
Acts 20:7 . . . . 85, 86	2 Timothy 3:16, 17. . . . . . 3, 51, 52
Acts 21:15 91	Hebrews 2:14. 88
Acts 22:16 87	Hebrews 13:8 79
Acts 28:13 91	James 2:24 84
Romans 1:16 81	James 3:13 91
Romans 3:23 83	1 Peter 1:24-25. . . . . 13, 38
Romans 5:12 . . . . 57, 58, 83	1 Peter 3:21 86
Romans 8:1 . . . . 61, 70	2 Peter 1:2 74
Romans 8:5 88	2 Peter 1:20-21. 3
Romans 10:13 . . . . 87, 88	1 John 5:7. . . . . 90, 91
Romans 10:14 45	2 John 12 85
1 Corinthians 2:9 83	Revelation 20:13-14. 90

Select Bibliography

Aland, Kurt, Matthew Black and Carlo M. Martini, et. al. *The Greek New Testament*. 3rd ed. Stuttgart: United Bible Societies, 1983.

Archer, Gleason L. and G.C. Chirichigno. *Old Testament Quotations in the New Testament: A Complete Survey*. Chicago: Moody Press, 1983.

Bettenson, Henry. *Documents of the Christian Church*. London: Oxford University Press, 1959.

____. *The Early Christian Fathers*. London: Oxford University Press, 1958.

Comfort, Philip W. *Early Manuscripts and Modern Translations of the New Testament*. Grand Rapids: Baker Books. 1990.

____ and David P. Barrett. *The Complete Text of the Earliest New Testament Manuscripts*. Grand Rapids: Baker Books. 1999.

Cross, F.L. and E.A. Livingstone. *The Oxford Dictionary of the Christian Church*. 2nd ed. New York: Oxford University Press, 1989.

Davies, Philip R., George J. Brooke, and Phillip R. Callaway. *The Complete World of the Dead Sea Scrolls*. London: Thames & Hudson, 2002.

Dowley, Tim. ed. *Eerdmans' Handbook to the History of Christianity*. Carmel, NY: William B. Eerdmans Publishing Co., 1977.

Finegan, Jack. *Encountering New Testament Manuscripts: A Working Introduction to Textual Criticism*. Grand Rapids: William B. Eerdmans Publishing Co., 1974.

Foster, Lewis. *Selecting a Translation of the Bible*. Cincinnati: Standard Pub., 1978.

Hodges, Zane C. and Arthur L. Farstad. *The Greek New Testament According to the Majority Text*. Nashville: Thomas Nelson Publishers, 1982.

Howard, David M. Jr. *Fascinating Bible Facts, People, Places & Events*. Lincolnville, IL: Publications Int. Ltd., 1992.

How We Got the Bible

Huber, Robert R. ed. *The Bible Through the Ages*. Pleasantville, NY: Reader's Digest Association, Inc., 1996.

Jobes, Karen H. and Moisés Silva. *Invitation to the Septuagint*. Grand Rapids: Baker Academics, 2000.

McDowell, Josh. *Evidence That Demands A Verdict*. San Bernardino, CA: Campus Crusade for Christ, 1979.

_____. *More Evidence That Demands A Verdict*. San Bernardino, CA: Campus Crusade for Christ, 1975.

_____ and Don Stewart. *Reasons Skeptics Should Consider Christianity*. San Bernardino, CA: Campus Crusade for Christ, 1981.

Metzger, Bruce. *A Textual Commentary on the Greek New Testament*. Stuttgart: United Bible Societies, 1971.

Mitchell, Edward C. *The Critical Handbook of the Greek New Testament*. New York: Harper and Brothers Pub., 1896.

Nestle, Eberhard, Erwin Nestle and Kurt Aland. *Novum Testmentum Graece*. 25 ed., Stuttgart: United Bible Societies, 1963.

Pache, René. *The Inspiration and Authority of Scripture*. Chicago: Moody Press, 1969.

Robinson, Maurice A. and William G. Perpont. Eds. *The New Testament in the Original Greek: Byzantine Textform*. Southborough, MA: Chilton Book Publishing, 2005.

Ryken, Leland. *Choosing a Bible: Understanding Bible Translation Differences*. Wheaton, IL: Crossway Books, 2005.

Scanlin, Harold. *The Dead Sea Scrolls & Modern Translations of the Old Testament*. Wheaton, IL: Tyndale House Publishers, 1993.

Sturz, Harry A. *The Byzantine Text-Type and New Testament Textual Criticism*. Nashville: Thomas Nelson Pub., 1984.

Van Leeuwen, Raymond C. "We Really Do Need Another Bible Translation," *Christianity Today*. October 22, 2001.

Visalli, Gayla. ed. *After Jesus: The Triumph of Christianity*. Pleasantville, NY: Reader's Digest Assoc. Inc., 1992.

Wegner, G.S. *6000 Years of the Bible*. NY: Harper and Row Pub., 1963.

www.ingramcontent.com/pod-product-compliance
Lightning Source LLC
Chambersburg PA
CBHW070854050426
42453CB00012B/2199